PROGRAMMING FOR BEGINNERS

THIS BOOK INCLUDES:

KALI LINUX AND PYTHON FOR BEGINNERS

ADAM HARRIS

Table of Contents

Kali linux:

Python for beginners:

Python for beginners:

KALI LINUX:

Introduction

Hacking is like cooking. You need to get ready with all the ingredients (i.e. programs) and know in detail about the properties of that ingredients (or programs) and use them together to produce a culinary material. What if the food doesn't taste good? That is if you are unable to get the better results after all the hacking process? There is only one way you can do i.e.; to try again.

There are five important areas you need to learn in detail to master hacking.

1) Information Gathering

2) Automatic Vulnerability Scanning

3) Exploiting

4) Password Attacks

5) Sniffing and wireless attacks

1) Information gathering

Information gathering is always considered a pivotal job hacker should do before attacking a target. It roughly sums up that by using information gathering tools we can acquire a lot of information about the target hosts, which can help us create exploits that would help us create a backdoor for further exploitation. We can even use tons of publicly available information about the target to get a good idea on what strategy we should use to make this attack successful.

2) Automatic Vulnerability scanning

Vulnerability Scanner is a program that automatically finds and discovers security vulnerabilities in computers, network applications, web applications and software. It detects the target system through the network, generates data to the target system, and matches the feedback data with the built-in vulnerability signature database to enumerate the security vulnerabilities existing on the target system. Vulnerability scanning is an indispensable means to ensure system and network security. In the face of Internet intrusion, if users can detect security vulnerabilities through network scanning as soon as possible according to the specific application environment, and timely take appropriate measures to repair, it can effectively prevent the occurrence of intrusion events. Because the work is relatively boring, we can implement it with some convenient tools, such as Nessus and OpenVAS.

3) Exploiting

Exploiting is an important way to gain control of the system. The user finds a vulnerable vulnerability from the target system and then uses the vulnerability to obtain permissions to control the target system. In order to facilitate the user's practice, this chapter will introduce Metasploitable 2 released by Metasploit. Users can use it as a Linux operating system for practice. This chapter will use the vulnerabilities on the Metasploitable system to introduce various penetration attacks, such as MySQL database, PostgreSQL database and Tomcat service.

Privilege escalation is to maximize the minimum privilege a user has. Often, the users we gain access to may have the lowest permissions. However, if you want to perform a penetration attack, you may need the administrator account permissions, so you need to increase the permissions. Permission elevation can be achieved by using fake tokens, local privilege escalation, and social engineering.

4) Password Attacks

A password attack is to recover the password plaintext without knowing the key. Password attacks are an important part of all penetration testing. If you are a penetration tester and don't understand passwords and password cracking, it's hard to imagine. So, no matter what you do or how far our technical capabilities are, passwords still seem to be the most common way to protect data and restrict access to the system. This chapter describes various password attack methods, such as password online attacks, router password attacks, and creating password dictionaries.

5) Sniffing and wireless attacks

This is where people use wireless network tools along with a network adapter to capture packets and crack password or acquire sensitive information from the target. Sniffing tools like Wireshark are famous and can be used for a lot of attacks and finding out the packets.

Information Gathering

Information gathering is an important pre attack phase where the hackers collect a lot of information that is available in public about the target he is going to attack. Many hackers use social engineering techniques to get a solid bunch of information about target and the technology it is using along with the operating system and version it uses. Every hacker uses different set of methodologies to create a good information about the host before targeting.

There are three important phases in information gathering as explained below

1) Gathering information from search engines

Use search engines like Google to get good information about the host you are trying to attack. You will be surprised with the fact that how much you can find information that is public.

2) Social engineering techniques

Social engineering techniques are crazy because you can just psychologically trick an employee or the target you are chasing with a simple thing like phishing email to create a backdoor via your exploit. All great hackers rely on social engineering instead of doing things in a more complex way.

3) Port Scanning

If you are curious to know about what a port scan is associated with follow the next few paragraphs carefully. There are various services provided by the server, such as publishing a home page and sending and receiving e-mails.

Services that perform network communication include a window called "port" for communication, which is managed by numbers. For example, well-known services are basically pre-assigned port numbers, such as 80 for HTTP services that publish their home pages on the Internet and 587 for sending emails.

The act of investigating from the outside (attacker point of view) that what kind of port the server is opening is called "port scan".

How a port scan be done?

Port scanning is the process of sending specific data from the outside and examining the corresponding responses in order to investigate the running services on servers connected to the network. By analyzing the response obtained, you can identify the version of the service running on the server, the OS, etc.

Nmap

Nmap is one of the famous hacking tools and is widely known for its popularity among penetration testers. People often mistake that Nmap is only popular for its information gathering abilities but often doesn't understand that Nmap can also be used as a vulnerability detector that can be automated. It can be used in various operating systems that are open source and in Windows.

Nmap is a powerful tool that can be used for port discovery, host discovery, service discovery, detection of operating system and its version. Nmap can be used in both command line and with graphical user interface (GUI). But remember that good hackers use the Command line.

How Nmap works?

Nmap is programmed in a way such that it can perform scanning using different technologies like TCP and FTP protocol scans. All these scans are prone to their strengths and weaknesses and hackers can understand it vividly when they are trying to attack hosts with Nmap.

In hacking terminology, we call the target technically as the target host. When using Nmap we need to first understand the complexity of target to decide which scan to use either simple easy scan or a complex scan that would take a lot more time. We need to polish our skills to use some very complex and intuitive techniques to get past from intrusion detection systems to get good results.

Below are some strategies that will help you appreciate various operations Nmap can perform:

1) You can scan a single host with the following command

nmap www.hackingtools.com

nmap 192.232.2.1

2) You can scan an entire subnet with the following command

nmap 192.232.2.1/24

3) Nmap can also be used to scan multiple targets with the following command

#nmap 192.232.2.1 192.232.2.4

4) There is also an option in Nmap that will let you scan a range of targets as follows

#nmap 192.232.2.1-100 (This in precise scans every host that is in between the IP addresses 192.232.2.1 and 192.232.2.100)

5) Nmap has an option where you can store all the Ip addresses you have in a text file that is in .txt format and place in the same directory of Nmap so that it can scan every IP address present in the text file without manually entering each one of them.

#nmap -iL sampleip.txt

6) If you want to see a list of all the hosts you need to scan you can enter the following command

#nmap -sL 192.232.2.1/24

7) Nmap provides an option where we can exclude a single IP address from scanning with subnet hosts

#nmap 192.232.2.1/24 -exclude 192.232.2.4

   And if you want to exclude more than one IP, you can include all of them in a text file so that they can be excluded while doing the subnet scan like shown below.

#nmap 192.232.2.1/24 -exclude excludeIp.txt

Before learning about the scanning procedures Nmap offers let us know about scanning ports on a specific host. You can scan individual ports in a host using the following command.

#nmap -p78,56,23 192.232.2.1

Scanning technology in Nmap

There are different types of scanning strategies that Nmap follows to do the work. In this section, we will describe about these procedures in detail along with few commands that will give you a good overview.

1) sS scan (Tcp SYN)

This is a typical scan that Nmap uses if nothing is specified by the hacker to the software. In this scan usually, Nmap will not give a full handshake to the target system. It will just send an SYN packet to the target host, which will then check for any open ports, but not creating any sessions that may be used after logging. This is one of the greatest strengths of this scanning strategy. To use this scan the hacking tool should be given root access otherwise it will show an error. Below we give the command line for this scan.

hacking@kali #nmap -sS 262.232.2.1

2) sT scan (TCP connect)

If the sS scan is not used due to the reason that it is not feasible for the current attack situation people normally use sT scan as their next savior. It gives three handshakes with open ports and calls a method called connect () which makes the software to find TCP ports. sT scan when preferred can also be used to find UDP ports although people use it rarely.

   Below is the command for -sT scan:

hacking @kali #nmap -sT 292.232.2.1

3) sU scan (UDP scan)

This scanning is also in the penetration-testing checklist after the importance of -sS scan. There is no need to send SYN packets like in TCP scan because this will just find UDP ports that are open. When the hackers start using the scan A UDP packet reaches the target host and waits for a positive response. If at all a response is received an open port is found. If it sends an error message with an Echo command then the port is closed.

Below is the command line for -sU scan

hacking @ kali #nmap -sU 292.232.2.1

4) sF scan (FIN scan)

This is a special type of scan that is used because some targets may have installed intrusion detection systems and firewalls that stop SYN packets that are sent using a TCP scan. For this sole reason, Fin scan is used if there is any extra detection scan happening on the other side. Fin scan does not save any log information to be detected so there is a great chance of the Fin packet to find out few open ports by sneaking into the target systems.

Here is the command for -sF scan

hacking@kali #nmap -sF 292.232.2.1

5) sP scan (Ping scan)

Ping is a famous network protocol method that checks whether a host is live or not by trying to connect to the target host. Ping scanning in Nmap also is used for the same purpose and is not used to check open ports. Ping scan asks for root access to start a scan. If you are not ready to provide the administrative privileges you can just use the connect method to start a ping sweep from Nmap.

Here is the command for -sP scan

hacking @ kali #nmap -sP 292.232.2.1

6) sV scan (version detection scan)

A version detection scan is one of the obsessive usages of Nmap for hackers. To attack a target system, you need to know about the technology and operating system the host is using so you create your exploits and backdoor strategies to break into the system. However, unlike TCP scans version detection scan takes a lot of time because when we start a sV scan in the background TCP scan gets started and searches for the open ports. After the hunt for open ports gets finished sV scan automatically analyzes them and determines the information about the target host. Due to this complex procedure, it may take a lot of time.

Here is the command for -sV scan

hacking @ kali #nmap -sV 292.232.2.1

7) sL scan (Idle scan)

This is one of the craziest features of Nmap because it just acts like a proxy server while doing attacks.

When using idle scan you can send packets using another host Ip. This anonymity can help hackers to stay in the dark if something goes wrong or severe. Protecting himself from the investigation is what every hacker strives for especially in these modern times.

Here is the command for -sL scan

hacking @ kali #nmap -sL 292.432.2.6 292.432.2.1

Things Nmap can detect:

Nmap can detect the Device type of the host that is (router, workgroup, etc.), running operating system, operating system details i.e. version and network distance (approximate distance between the target and the attacker).

While using Nmap always use ping scan only when necessary because some firewalls in the target hosts can detect that an attack is going to happen and will block the attacker's addresses to make any connection.

By using the below command you are saying to the software that doesn't ping the remote host:

hacking @ kali # nmap -O -PN 292.428.5.6/ 12

Using the-PN parameter can bypass the Ping Command, but it does not affect the discovery of the host system. NMAP operating system detection is based on open and closed ports. If Os scan cannot detect at least one open or closed port, it will return the following error.

The error code is below:

Warning: we cannot find any open or closed ports to get information on the target system

It is difficult to accurately detect the remote operating system with NMAP, so we need to use NMAP's guess function, osscan-guess operation guesses which operating system type is closest to the target.

#nmap -O -osscan -guess 192.232.2.1

Before going to talk about Nessus let us have a simple exercise. Please try to do this Exercise for better understanding of the Information Gathering.

Exercise:

Start kali Linux terminal and enter into Nmap using the commands. Find the subnet masks for www.nmap.com and find the operating system and version that it uses. Complete different scans and create a detailed report on all the ports that are available.

Chapter 1 How to Setup and Install Kali Linux a USB Key

Kali Linux is the best hacking tool out there. It is super secure, and it is made by seasoned professionals who know what they are doing. What's so great about this system is that you can run it from a USB key and not have to worry about compromising or altering your current operating system. When you carry this OS on a USB key, it can be taken to any computer or compatible device and made to work. It only temporarily overrides the current operating system on that device.

Once you take out your USB key, you remove Kali Linux from the device. It doesn't leave behind any trace, and it doesn't change the settings or operating system of the device you used it on. It is compatible with any operating system because it works around them.

This is considered a non-destructive way to use Kali Linux. It lets everything go back to normal on whatever device you use it on, making no changes to the host's system. It's also portable, so you can take it from one workstation to the next and from one device to the next and do what you need to do. It starts up very fast, usually in just a few minutes, on whatever system you put it into.

You can also customize your bootable drive, using a Kali Linux ISO image that you rolled yourself. It is also potentially persistent. This means that, once you perform the proper configurations, your Kali Linux Live drive will keep the data it has collected no matter how many times you reboot it.

Installing onto Your Bootable USB Key

For Windows users, you will have to first download the Win32 Disk Imager utility. You'll find that <u>here</u>.

https://launchpad.net/win32-image-writer

If you are using a Linux or an OS X, just use the dd command. This has already been installed on both of th§ose platforms.

We recommend using a 4GB USB thumb drive or larger. If you want to use an SD card, then that's fine, since the procedure is the same for both. Just make sure the devices you are going to be using it on are compatible with your storage device.

The method for doing this will differ depending on what OS you have. We'll break it down on both of the major ones for you.

For Windows

Start by plugging your USB drive into a USB port on a PC operating Windows. Pay attention to the drive designator that it uses when it starts to mount. That designator will look like "F:\". Then launch the Win32 Disk Imager software. Once you open that software, pick out the Kali Linux ISO file you downloaded. Then click "Write" to copy it onto the USB drive, be sure you pick the right drive for this operation.

When the imaging process is finished, you can take out your USB. On most Windows OS, you will need to click on the small arrow near the bottom right corner of your screen to open a tab that shows connected devices. Be sure to click on your USB drive there to safely eject it and ensure that no information is lost when you disconnect it.

Once all that is done, you can boot Kali Linux from your USB device.

For Linux

Doing the same thing on a Linux is equally easy. Start with the verified ISO image and copy it over to the drive using the dd command. You have to be running as a root for this to work. Alternatively, you can execute the dd command using sudo. The instructions we're going to give you assume that you have a Linux Mint 17.1 desktop. Other versions are going to vary slightly, but the basic operations required for this task should all be about the same.

Just a word of warning before we get into the actual instruction: if you aren't sure what you are doing with dd command or you just aren't careful, you can accidently overwrite something you aren't meaning to. Be sure to double check everything you are doing so you don't make any mistakes.

Start by identifying the device path you are going to use to write the image onto the USB drive. Before the drive is inserted, perform the command "sudo fdisk -1"

You have to be using elevated privileges with fdisk, otherwise there won't be any output. Enter the above command in a terminal window at a command prompt. If you did it properly, you should see a single drive. That will probably look like this "/dev/sda". That drive will be separated into three partitions. These are /dev/sda1, /dev/sda2, and /dev/sda5.

From there, plug in the USB drive, then run the original command again. That's sudo fdisk -1. Once you do that, you will see another device that wasn't there initially. It could look something like this: "/dev/sdb".

Then take the ISO file and image it onto the USB device. It may take 10-15 minutes to image the USB device, so be patient. In order to perform this process, you need to execute the command below:

dd   if=kali-linux-1.0.9a-amd32.iso   of=/dev/sdb bs=512k

Let's dissect this command for a second. In the example we are using here, the ISO image that you want to write onto the drive is named "kali-linux-1.0.9a-amd32.iso". Yours may look slightly different. Note the "32" in the name. This refers to the size of the image. We use the blocksize value "bs=512k" because it is safe and reliable. You can make it bigger if you want, but that can cause some problems, so it isn't recommended.

Once the command is completed, then it will provide feedback and not before then. Your drive could have an access indicator. If it does, then it will blink every so often. How long this whole process takes will depend on a few factors- how fast your system is, what kind of USB drive you are using and how well your USB port works. The output, once the imaging is complete, will tell you how many bytes are copied and give you numbers for records in and out, which should be the same number.

Now your USB is ready to boot into a Kali Live environment.

Chapter 1 Darknet Markets

Just how safe is a Darknet in light of the vulnerabilities discussed? The short answer is, *as safe as you make it.*

You are the weak link. The last link in the security chain. And although you need Tor to access Onion sites, the term can apply to any anonymous network - networks like I2P or Freenet or anything else that cloaks the source of data transmit, and by extension, your identity.

Which brings us to the *Darknet Marketplace*.

The complete list of such marketplaces on the deep web are numerous, and the risk of getting scammed is quite high. It's one reason why you may not have heard about them. They are often taken down quickly by either a venomous reputation or a law enforcement bust. Sometimes they piss off the wrong people and then spammers ddos the site. But there are numerous places one can go if you're curious about what is sold by whom.

When I say *sold*, what I mean is, anything you want that cannot be gained through the usual legal channels. And remember that what is legal in one country may be illegal in another. In Canada, lolicon comics are illegal and can get you in big trouble if you cross the border. But not in America. In the USA you can pretty much write any story you want. In Canada? TEXT stories involving minors are verboten.

The other difference is that there are safety nets in buying almost anything in a first world country on the open market. Think BestBuy. Mom and Pop stores. Florist shops. If customers get injured, what happens? Customers sue via the legal safety net and make a lot of lawyers a lot of money.

But the Darknet Marketplace laughs at any such safety nets. In fact, you're likely to get scammed at least a few times before finding a reputable dealer for whatever goods you seek. And it really doesn't matter what it is, either - Teleportation devices? Pets? Exotic trees? It's all the same that goes around. Whatever is in demand will attract unsavory types and not just on the buyer's end.

Therefore, research any darknet market with Tor, being careful to visit forums and check updated information to see if any sites have been flagged as suspicious or compromised. Some other advice:

- Always use PGP to communicate.

- Never store crypto-currency at any such marketplace.

- Assume a den of thieves unless proven otherwise by *them*. The responsibility is theirs just as it is offline, to prove they are an honest business. If you open your own, keep this in mind: customers owe you nothing. You can only betray them once.

Now for some examples of Phishers and Scammers and other Con men. By their fruits, ye shall know them.

1.) <u>SILK ROAD 2.0</u> *(e5wvymnx6bx5euvy...)* Lots of scams with this one. Much like Facebook and Google emails, you can tell a fake sometimes by the address. Paste the first few letters into a shortcut next to the name. If it doesn't match, steer clear.

2.) **Green Notes Counter**
(67yjqewxrd2ewbtp...)
They promised counterfeit money to their customers but refuse escrow. A dead giveaway.

3.) iPhones for half off: (IPHONEAVZHWKQMAP...)

Now here is a prime example of a scam. Any website which sells electronic gadgets on the deep web is ripe for scamming customers. Whereas in the Far East you will merely get counterfeit phones with cheap, Chinese made parts that break within a month, on the Deep Web they will simply take your money and say adios. Actually, they won't even bother saying that.

So then, how does one tell a scam?

Because many new darknet vendors will arise out of thin air, with rare products that will make customers swoon and send them money - without doing any research on their name or previous sales. A real hit and run operation. Hit quick and fast and dirty. Seduce as many as they can before the herd catches on to the wolf in disguise. Many are suckered, thinking "it's only a little money, but a little money from a lot of Tor users goes a long way in encouraging other scammers to set up shop.

When you ask them why they do not offer escrow, they say "We think it is unreliable/suspicious/unstable" amid other BS excuses. It is better to hold on to your small change than leave a trail to your treasure chest. And make no mistake some of these scammers are like bloodhounds where identity theft is concerned.

Do your research! Check forums and especially the dates of reviews they have. Do you notice patterns? Are good reviews scattered over a long period of time or is it rather all of a sudden--the way some Amazon affiliate marketers do with paid reviews that glow? Not many reviews from said customers?

If you've seen the movie "Heat," with Al Pacino and Robert de Niro, you know when it is time to Walk Away. In the middle of a nighttime heist, Niro goes outside for a smoke. He hears a distant cough. Somewhere. Now, this is middle of the night in an unpopulated part of the city that comes from across the street - a parking lot full of what he thought were empty trailers. Hmm, he thinks maybe this isn't such a great night for a hot score. Not so empty (it was a cop in a trailer full of other hotshot cops). He walks back into the bank and tells his partner to abort.

The other aspect is time. Some fake sites will set a short ship time and count on you not bothering to see the sale as finalized before you can whistle Dixie out of your ass. After finalization, you're screwed since the money is in their wallet before you can even mount a protest.

Fraud Prevention

One is Google believe it or not, at

http://www.google.com/imghp.

Dating sites like Cherry Blossoms and Cupid sometimes use reverse image search to catch fakers and Nigerian scammers masquerading as poor lonely singles to deprive men of their coinage. If they can catch them, so can you. If the image belongs to some other legit site, chances are it is fake. **Foto Forensics** also does the same, and reports metadata so that it becomes even harder to get away with Photoshop trickery.

When it is Okay to FE (Finalize Early)

FE means 'Finalize Early'. It's use online can usually be found in black marketplaces like Silk Road and Sheep's Marketplace. It simply means that money in escrow is released before you receive your product. Every customer I've ever spoken with advises against this unless you've had great experience with that business.

But... quite a few vendors are now making it a *standard practice* to pay funds up front before you have anything in your hands.

On more than one Marketplace forum, there's been heated exchange as to when this is proper. You might hear, "Is this guy legit? What about this Chinese outfit over here? He seems shady," and others: "A friend said this guy is okay but then I got ripped off!". You get the idea.

Here is my experience on the matter.

1.) It is okay when you are content with not getting what you paid for. This may seem counterproductive, but think how many gamblers go into a Las Vegas casino and never ask themselves "How much can I afford to lose?"

The answer, sadly, is not many. Vegas was not built on the backs of losers. Some merchants do not like escrow at all. Some do. So don't spend more than you can afford to lose. Look at it the way a gambler looks at making money.

2.) It is okay when you are guaranteed shipment. There are FE scammers out there that will give you an angelic smile and lie right into your eyes as they swindle you. Do not depend solely on reviews. A guy on SR can be the best merchant this side of Tatooine and yet you will wake up one day and find yourself robbed. He's split with a million in BTC and you're left not even holding a bag. Most won't do this to you. But a few will.

When it is NOT Okay to FE

When losing your funds will result in you being evicted or a relationship severed. Never borrow money from friends and especially not family unless you want said family to come after you with a double-bladed ax. If you get ripped off, you lose not only the cash but the respect and trustworthiness of your family. Word spreads. You don't pay your debts. What's that saying in Game of Thrones?

Right. A Lannister always pays his debts. So should you.

MultiSigna

Sounds like something from Battlestar Galactica to pass from ship to ship. A badge of honor perhaps some hotshot flyboy wears on his fighter jacket that bypassed a lot of red tape.

While not exactly mandatory, it makes for interesting reading, and is something Tor users might want to know about if they wish to make purchases anonymously. Here's what happens:

When a purchase is enacted, the seller deposits money (in this case, Bitcoins) in a multi-signature address. After this, the customer gets notification to make the transaction ($,€) to the seller's account.

Then after the seller relays to MultiSigna that the transaction was a success, MultiSigna creates a transaction from the multi-signature address that requires both buyer and seller so that it may be sent to the network. The buyer gets the Bitcoins and ends the sale. Confused yet? I was too at first. You'll get used to it.

Critical

MultiSigna only exists as a verifier/cosigner of the entire transaction. If there is disagreement between seller and buyer, NO EXCHANGE occurs. Remember the scene in Wargames when two nuclear silo operators have to turn their keys simultaneously in order to launch? Yeah, that.

MultiSigna will of course favor one or the other, but not both if they cannot mutually agree. The upside is that is if the market or purchaser or vendor loses a key, two out of three is still available. A single key cannot spend the money in 2/3 MultiSig address.

Is it Safe? Is it Secret?

I don't recommend enacting a million dollar exchange for a yacht, or even a thousand dollar one as they both carry risk, but ultimately it is up to you.

Just remember that trust is always an issue on darknets, and you're generally safer making several transfers with a seller/buyer who has a good history of payment. In other words, reputation as always, is everything.

Alas, there are a few trustworthy markets that have good histories of doing things properly, thank heavens.

Blackbank is one. **Agora** is another. Take a look at the Multi-Sig Escrow Onion page here with Tor:

http://u5z75duioy7kpwun.onion/wiki/index.php/Multi-Sig_Escrow

Security

What the effect would be if a hacker gained entry to the server? What mischief might he make? What chaos could he brew if he can mimic running a withdrawal in the same manner that the server does?

If a hacker were to gain access and attempt to withdraw money, a single-signature would be applied and passed to the second sig signer for co-signature. Then the security protocol would kick in where these policies would be enforced:

1.) Rate limits: the rate of stolen funds slows

2.) Callbacks to the spender's server: Signing service verifies with the original spender that they initiated and intended to make the spend. The callback could go to a separated machine, which could only contain access to isolated approved withdrawal information.

3.) IP limiting: The signing service only signs transactions coming from a certain list of IPs, preventing the case where the hacker or insider stole the private key.

4.) Destination Whitelists: Certain very high security wallets can be set such that the signing service would only accept if the destination were previously known. The hacker would have to compromise both the original sending server as well as the signing service.

Let me repeat that MultiSigna are *never in possession* of your bitcoins. They use 2 of 3 signatures (seller, buyer & MultiSigma) to sign a transaction. Normal transactions are signed by the seller and then by the buyer.

Purchaser Steps for MultiSig Escrow

1.) Deposit your Bitcoins. Purchase ability is granted after 6 confirmations

2.) Make a private & public key (Brainwallet.org is a JavaScript Client-Side Bitcoin Address Generator)

3.) Buy item, input public-key & a refund BTC address

4.) Retrieve purchased item

5.) Input the private key and close

Chapter 2 Web Security

In this chapter, we will briefly talk about web security and about some attacks that you need to have in mind. I'm absolutely sure you've heard a lot of times on TV, radio or from other sources of the company's X site being broken, the organization's Y site being down and hackers replacing the main site with a fake page.

Well, I want to tell you that at large (Less Experienced Hackers) they all look for many vulnerabilities well known to their sites 1 to 2 that they can take advantage of. There are many tools that help them locate these vulnerabilities relatively easily, and then help them exploit them.

Some of these vulnerabilities (web-level) are extremely well presented and documented in the Open Web Application Security Project (*OWASP*). OWASP is a nonprofit organization dedicated to improving the security of software and web applications.

They have a *top 10* with the most commonly reported security incidents in previous years on websites and web applications. OWASP organizes even local events (you can research on Google or Facebook for such events), creating a community of passionate cyber security people.

If you hear at some point of such an event and you have the opportunity to go, I recommend you to take this step because you will see that it is worthwhile first and secondly that you learn a lot of things from many people.

As you can see for the most part, it's about the same type of vulnerabilities, with the top changing very little over a three-year period. We will only take some of these attacks and explain to you what each person represents and how you can do them on your own site.

Here are the attacks, we will discuss further:

- SQL injection

- **XSS**

- Security Misconfiguration

Now let's start talking about web attacks with the first attack / vulnerability (and most common) from the list above:

1) SQL Injection

When we talk about SQL injection, we are talking primarily about databases, and secondly about the attack (a vulnerability) at their level. Let's first look at what SQL is. *SQL (Structured Query Language)* is a query language with databases. It is used to communicate directly with the database through various commands addressed to it. There are several types / forms of SQL, but the basics are the same.

Where are the SQL injection attacks? Most often these occur when the attacker finds a "box" in which he can enter data. For example, think about a search box in which anyone can write anything.

If the back code (most often PHP) is not written properly, then the hacker can enter SQL commands that interact directly with the database, so they can extract different information.

Now I want you to think that when you interact with an "input form" (a box where you can write and send something to the server), this happens:

That is, PHP language will generate such an order to interact (and search) with the database. In the place where '%' appears, it will be replaced with what you enter in that input form.

Here's an example of a SQL code that can be entered in this field (ATTENTION: it will not work for any site. I suggest using the bWAPP application and testing it):

```
' OR 1=1;--
```

You can try on **this site** (https://sqlzoo.net/hack/) to enter the SQL statement above instead of the username and password.

SQLmap (http://sqlmap.org/) is a great tool you can use to *test database vulnerabilities* on a site. SQLmap will do all these queries that automatically automate SQL injection for you (and even try to break the hash of the passwords you will find in the database).

Another reason why WordPress is so used is due to the number of existing plugins that can be used to improve the site, user experience, etc. So the person who manages a site / blog using such a CMS does NOT need programming skills because the plugins deal (mostly) with everything that's needed. There are over 50,000 free plugins available in the WordPress marketplace, and besides these, the paid ones that have been developed by different companies.

Another very interesting aspect related to WordPress is that he is Open Source. This means it is developed by a community of programmers to whom anyone can take part.

As running technologies, WordPress needs *LAMP* (*Linux, Apache, MySQL, PHP*). Each of these components is critical in running a site. If you are not familiar with LAMP I will briefly explain what each component is:

> 1. *Linux* - The OS on which the site will work, the reason being simple: a flexible,

stable OS and more secure than Windows

2.*Apache* - The web server used to host the site, most widespread in the Internet

3.*MySQL* - The database used by WordPress to store the information site (articles,

users, comments and any other type of content that requires storage)

4.*PHP* - The programming language that interacts with each component (base data, web server and OS). PHP is a web programming language used on the backhand side (what we do not see when we access a site)

If you want to install WordPress for your own use, you will need a web hosting server. I recommend you USE THIS ONE (BLUEHOST) - http://bit.ly/2HvO3je- (which provides you with 1-click install so you can start immediately using your WordPress site.

Now, after installing WordPress, I suggest we move on to a security scanning tool for your website.

WPScan

WPScan is a scan tool (and of course a crack) of a WordPress-based site. It is open source, so it can be used by anyone who wants to test their site for vulnerabilities. This tool can give you a lot of information about your site:

- The WordPress version used (a very good indicator)
- Plugins installed
- Potential vulnerabilities existing on the site, which can then be exploited
- Finding existing users on the site
- Making Brute Force attacks by using a password finder

Often, scanning can be perceived as actively testing your system to see what you can find through it. You can compare this concept to the one in which someone (stranger) wants to "see" what you have in the house. Enter the door (without you being home) and start looking through your things, but do not take anything in order to use that information later.

Makes a non-intrusive scan ():

 # wpscan --url www.example.com

Enumerates (lists) the installed plugins:

 # wpscan --url www.example.com -- enumerate p

Runs all enumeration tools in order to learn as much information as possible:

 # wpscan --url www.example.com -- enumerate

List the existing users on the site:

 # wpscan --url www.example.com -- enumerate u

These are some ways to use the WPScan tool. In below, I placed my first order on a WordPress-based site (whose identity I will not publish) to see what information we can find out about it. I mention that I was authorized to do such a scan on this site.
And from a simple scan of how many vulnerabilities I found on this site (he definitely needs an update). As you see, there are many vulnerabilities that can be exploited using different methods. Moreover, there are also these **CVE**S (*Common Vulnerability and Exposures*) https://www.cvedetails.com/browse-by-date.php that describe the vulnerability and how it can be exploited.

Because we're talking about WordPress and *vulnerabilities* after all, **HERE** (https://wpvulndb.com/) you can see a database that contains all the *vulnerabilities known* and made *public* for each version. In addition to this, I want to tell you that all the attacks, we have talked about in this chapter also apply to the WordPress case. Unfortunately, *SQLi, XSS, Traversal Directory* are only a few (of many) attacks that can be done relatively easily on this platform. With WPScan all you do is find them much faster.

It's important *to be aware* of them, to frequently scan your website (yourself or a client), discover new vulnerabilities, and do them to resolve them as quickly as possible.

5) Google Hacking

I think you had a slightly different reaction when you saw the title of this topic: "Wow! can I hack up Google?" or "can I hack with Google?" I can tell you yes, in the 2nd situation (although the first is not excluded: D). You can use Google to discover different sites that have certain *pages indexed* in the search engine. Thus, using a few specific search keywords, Google can give you exactly what you are looking for (*sites* that contain exactly the *URL* you are looking for with a vulnerable plug-in, a database information page like that be the user, the password and the name of the database, etc.).

Yes, site administrators are not mindful (probably not even aware) of their site being able to *leak valuable information on Google*, making it extremely exposed to Internet attacks.

Again, I give you this information because you can use it for ethical purposes (to research and test your site or that of a customer). Do not forget that unauthorized access to a system will be penalized and you may take a few years in prison for this (I know a few people who have suffered this ...).

Now that you have remembered this, here are some examples where you can do a research. With this search, Google will display sites that have a WordFence plugin (a site security plug-in - firewall, virus scanner, etc.)

inurl:"/wp-content/plugins/wordfence/"
This was just one example (in). Of course you can replace search content by "*inurl:*" with whatever you want, depending on your current interest.

By following the order in Google Search, you will be able to see different sites depending on the version of WordPress they use. Then you can use WPScan and find out more about the vulnerabilities that exist on it, then you can try to take advantage of it (ethically). You will see that there are many very old, extremely vulnerable versions of WordPress. What I recommend you is to get in touch with the site admin, to make him aware that he is exposed to a massive risk and to ask him to let you prove it (that is, attacking his site) : D).

inurl:"wordpress readme.html"

Chapter 3 Information Gathering Tools

The beginning of any attacks initiates from the stage of information gathering. When you gather as much information about the target, the attack becomes an easy process. Having information about the target also results in a higher success rate of the attack. A hacker finds all kinds of information to be helpful.

The process of information gathering includes:

1. Gathering information that will help in social engineering and ultimately in the attack

2. Understanding the range of the network and computers that will be the targets of the attack

3. Identifying and understanding all the complete surface of the attack i.e. processes and systems that are exposed

4. Identifying the services of a system that are exposed, and collecting as much information about them as possible

   5. Querying specific service that will help fetch useful data such as usernames

We will now go through Information Gathering tools available in Kali Linux one by one.

Nmap and Zenman

Ethical hacking is a phase in Kali Linux for which the tools NMap and ZenMap are used. NMap and ZenMap are basically the same tool. ZenMap is a Graphical Interface for the NMap tool which works on the command line.

The NMap tool which is for security auditing and discovery of network is a free tool. Apart from penetration testers, it is also used by system administrators and network administrators for daily tasks such as monitoring the uptime of the server or a service and managing schedules for service upgrades.

NMap identifies available hosts on a network by using IP packets which are raw. This also helps NMap identify the service being hosted on the host which includes the name of the application and the version. Basically, the most important application it helps identify on a network is the filter or the firewall set up on a host.

Stealth Scan

The Stealth scan is also popularly known as the hal open scan or SYN. It is called the half open scan because it refrains from completing the usual three-way handshake of TCP. So how it works is a SYN packet is sent by an attacker to the target host. The target host will acknowledge the SYN and sent a SYN/ACK in return. If a SYN/ACK is received, it can be safely assumed that the connection to the target host will complete and the port is open and listening on the target host. If the response received is RST instead, it is safe to assume that the port is close or not active on the target host.

acccheck

The acccheck tool was developed has an attack tool consisting of a password dictionary to target Windows Authentication processes which use the SMB protocol. The accccheck is basically a wrapper script which is injected in the binary of 'smbclient' and therefore depends on the smbclient binary for execution.

Server Message Block (SMB) protocol is an implementation of Microsoft for file sharing over a network and is popularly known as the Microsoft SMB Protocol.

It was then extended to the SMB "Inter-Process Communication" (IPC) system which implements named pipes and was one of the first inter process services that programmers got access to and which served as a means of inheritance for multiple services for authentication as they would all use the same credentials as that which were keyed in for the very first connection to the SMB server.

Amap

Amap is a scanning too of the next generation that allows a good number of options and flags in its command line syntax making it possible to identify applications and processes even if the ports that they are running on are different.

For example, a web server by default accepts connections on port 80. But most companies may change this port to something else such as 1253 to make the server secure. This change would be easily discovered by Amap.

Furthermore, if the services or applications are not based on ASCII, Amap is still able to discover them. Amap also has a set of interesting tools, which have the ability to send customized packets which will generate specific responses from the target host.

Amap, unlike other network tools is not just a simple scanner, which was developed with the intention of just pinging a network to detect active hosts on the network. Amap is equipped with amapcrap, which is a module that sends bogus and completely random data to a port. The target port can be UDP, TCP, SSL, etc. The motive is to force the target port to generate a response.

CaseFile

A huge number of Maltegousers were using Maltego to try and build graphical data from offline investigations and that is how CaseFile was born. Since there was no need of the transform provided by Maltego and the real need was just the graphing capability of Maltego in and more flexible way, CaseFile was developed.

CaseFile, being an application of visual intelligence, helps to determine the relationships, connections and links in the real world between information of different types. CaseFile lets you understand the connections between data that may apart from each other by multiple degrees of separation by plotting the relationships between them graphically. Additionally, CaseFile comes bundled with many more entities that are useful in investigations making it a tool that is efficient. You can also add your custom entities to CaseFile, which allows you to extend this tool to your own custom data sets.

braa

Braa is a tool that is used for scanning mass Simple Network Management Protocol (SNMP). The tool lets you make SNMP queries, but unlike other tools which make single queries at a time to the SNMP service, braa has the capability to make queries to multiple hosts simultaneously, using one single process. The advantage of braa is that it scans multiple hosts very fast and that too by using very limited system resources.

Unlike other SNMP tools, which require libraries from SNMP to function, braa implements and maintains its own stack of SNMP. The implementation is very complex and dirty. Supports limited data types, and cannot be called up to standard in any case. However braa was developed to be a fast tool and it is fast indeed.

dnsmap

dnsmap is a tool that came into existence originally in 2006 after being inspired from the fictional story "The Thief No One Saw" by Paul Craig.

A tool used by penetration testers in the information gathering stage, dnsmap helps discover the IP of the target company, domain names, netblocks, phone numbers, etc.

Dnsmap also helps on subdomain brute forcing which helps in cases where zone transfers of DNS do not work. Zone transfers are not allowed publicly anymore nowadays which makes dnsmap the need of the hour.

DotDotPwn

The dotdotpwn tool can be defined simply to call it a fuzzer. What is a fuzzer? A fuzzer is a testing tool that targets software for vulnerabilities by debugging and penetrating through it. It scans the code and looks for flaws and loopholes, bad data, validation errors, parameters that may be incorrect and other anomalies of programming.

Whenever an anomaly is encountered by the software, the software may become unresponsive, making way for the flaws to give an open door to an attack. For example, if you are an attacker whose target is a company's web server, with the help of dotdotpwn, you will be able to find a loophole in the code of the web server. Perhaps there has been a latest HTTP update on the server overnight. Using a fuzzer on the web server shows you there is an exploit with respect to data validation which leaves an open door for a DoS attack. You can now exploit this vulnerability, which will make the server crash and server access will be denied to genuine employees of the company. There are many such errors that can be discovered using a fuzzer and it is very common for technology to have error when it releases something new in the market and it takes time to identify the error and fix it.

Another example would be an attack with respect to SQL called SQLi where 'i' stands for injection. SQL injection attacks are achieved by injecting SQL database queries through web forms that are available on a website. The conclusion is that software will always be vulnerable allowing attackers to find a way to break their way into the system.

Fierce

Fierce is a Kali tool which is used to scan ports and map networks. Discovery of hostnames across multiple networks and scanning of IP spaces that are non-contiguous can be achieved by using Fierce. It is a tool much like Nmap but in case of Fierce, it is used specifically for networks within a corporate.

Once the target network has been defined by a penetration tester, Fierce runs a whole lot of tests on the domains in the target network and retrieves information that is valuable and which can be analyzed and exploited by the attacker.

Fierce has the following features.

- Capabilities for a brute-force attack through custom and built-in test list

- Discovery of nameservers

- Zone transfer attacks

- Scan through IP ranges both internal and external

- Ability to modify the DNS server for reverse host lookups

Wireshark

Wireshark is a kali too that is an open source analyzer for network and works on multiple platforms such as Linux, BSD, OS X and Windows.

It helps one understand about the functioning of a network thus making it of use in government infrastructure, education industries and other corporates.

It is similar to the tcpdump tool, but WIreshark is a notch above as it has a graphical interface through which you can filter and organize the data that has been captured, which means that it takes less time to analyze the data further. There is also an only text based version known as tshark, which has almost the same amount of features.

Wireshark has the following features.

-       The interface has a user-friendly GUI

-       Live capture of packets and offline analysis

-       Support for Gzip compression and extraction

-       Inspection of full protocol

-       Complete VOiP analysis

-       Supports decryption for IPsec, Kerberos, SSL/TLS, WPA/WPA2
                    URLCrazy

URLCrazy is a Kali tool that can that tests and generates typos and variations in domains to target and perform URL hijacking, typo squatting and corporate espionage. It has a database that can generate variants of up to 15 types for domains, and misspellings of up to 8000 common spellings. URLCrazy supports a variety of keyboard layouts, checks if a particular domain is in use and figures how popular a typo is.

The Harvester

The Harvester is a Kali tool that is not your regular hacking tool. Whenever there is a mention of hacking tools that are implemented using the command line, one usually thinks of tools like Nmap, Reaver, Metasploit and other utilities for wireless password cracking. However, the harvester refrains from using algorithms that are advanced to break into firewalls, or crack passwords, or capture the data of the local network.

Instead, the Harvester simply gathers publicly available information such as employee names, email addresses, banners, subdomains and other information in the same range. You may wonder as to why it collects this data. Because this data is very useful in the primary stage of information gathering. All this data helps study and understand the target system which makes attacking easier for the hacker or the penetration tester.

Furthermore, it helps the attacker understand as to how big and Internet footprint the target has. It also helps organizations to know how much publicly available information their employees have across the Internet. The latest version of the Harvester has updates which lets it keep intervals between the requests it makes to pages on the Internet, improves search sources, plotting of graphs and statistics, etc.

The Harvester crawls through the Internet as your surrogate, looking for information on your behalf as long as the criteria provided by you matches the information on the Internet. Given that you can also gather email addresses using the Harvester, this tool can be very useful to a hacker who is trying to penetrate an online login by gaining access to the email account of an individual.

Metagoofil

Metagoofil is a kali tool that is aimed at fetching publicly available such as pdf, xls, doc, ppt, etc. documents of a company on the Internet.

The tool makes a Google search to scan through documents and download them to the local machine. It then extracts the metadata of the documents using libraries such as pdfminer, hachoir, etc. It then feeds the information gathering process with the results of its report which contains usernames, server or machine names and software version which helps penetration testers with their investigation.

Miranda

Miranda is a Kali tool that is actively or passively used to detect UPnP hosts, its services, its devices and actions, all through on single command. The Service state parameters and their associated actions are correlated automatically and are then processed as input/output variables for every action. Miranda uses a single data structure to store information of all the hosts and allows you access to that data structure and all its contents.

Let's discuss what exactly ÚPnP is. Universal Plug and Play or UPnP is a protocol for networking that allows devices on the network such as computers, printers, routers mobile devices, etc. to discover each other seamlessly over a network and established services between them for sharing of data, entertainment and other communication. It is ideally for networks inside a private residence as opposed to corporate infrastructure.

Ghost Phisher

Ghost Phisher is a Kali tool, which is used as an attack software program and also for security auditing of wired and wireless networks. It is developed using the Python programming language and the Python GUI library. The program basically emulates access points of a network therefore, deploying its own internal server into a network.

Fragroute

Fragroute is a Kali tool that is used for intercepting, modifying and rewriting traffic that is moving toward a specific host. Simply put, the packets from attacking system known as frag route packets are routed to the destination system. It is used for bypassing firewalls mostly by attackers and security personnel. Information gathering is a well-known use case for fragroute as well which used by penetration testers who use a remote host, which is highly secured.

Masscan

Masscan is a Kali tool, which is used by penetration testers all around the world and has been in the industry for a long time. It is a tool of reconnaissance which has the capability to transmit up to 10 million packets every second. The transmission used by masscan is asynchronous and it has custom stack of TCP/IP. Therefore, the threads used for sending and receiving packets are unique.

Masscan is used to simultaneously attack a large number of hosts and that too quickly. The tool developer claims that masscan can scan the entire Internet in 6 minutes. Given its super high transmission rate, it has a use case in the domain of stress testing as well.

However, to achieve those high transmission rates, special drives and NICs are required. The communication of the tool with the users is very similar to that between the user and the Nmap tool.

Feature of masscan are as follows.

- It can be used to enumerate the whole Internet

- It can be used to enumerate a huge number of hosts

- Various subnets within an organization can be enumerated

- It can be used for random scanning and fun on the Internet

Chapter 4 Advanced Kali Linux Concepts

Using abusive services

Services are the most important mechanisms that Linux operates for a better functioning of the operating system. Even windows have services that run-in background. Basically, services are processes that run in the background until you use it. For example, consider a proxy server like Burp suite that will intercept every information that goes on in the browser and if you click No it stops the service and nothing goes there. In windows, which is quite well dominated by graphical user, interfaces services are easily closed down by a click. Whereas in Linux we need to start using command line to start, stop and restart services.

Why services matter to hackers?

Hackers should be well learnt about services because when you are trying to exploit a system you need to stop services that can interrupt what you are doing. Clever administrators use services to make hackers confuse. So, you need to understand the services that are making your exploitation difficult and stop them as soon as possible. Some advanced hackers install their own services after exploiting the system in a way that they will receive valuable information from the host regularly. In the below section we will explain with command line examples that will help us understand dealing with services.

1) Starting a Service

To start burp suite as a service go to Linux terminal as a root user and just use the following command.

root @ kali:service burpsuite start

This will start the service and you can check it using the ps command.

2) Stopping a Service

Stopping a service will completely abort everything that service is dealing with. So always, be careful while stopping a service as any unsaved data will be lost. Now use the following command to stop the service.

root @ kali:service burpsuite stop

You can check using ps command where you will not see anything related to burpsuit service.

3) Restarting a Service

Restarting a service just reboots everything about a particular service. Data will be lost and new service arises all on its own.

root @ kali:service burpsuit restart

This can be used when any service is struck or stops abruptly.

Now in this below section we will use the Apache web server and MySQL to explain how services can be useful for a hacker. This is a very basic and introductory level of abusing services. If you are an efficient hacker, you will understand hundreds of services and will try to learn about them in time and time to be a professional. Now let us start exploring these below services.

1) Apache Web server:

Apache is a famous web server that is being used by several hosting companies for deploying their web services. It is a well known open source web server that is well structured and of good security. We will use this apache web server to learn a few things that can help us as a hacker.

Step 1: Starting Apache

Apache webserver can be started using the following command. Normally in windows and Hosting environment there will be a GUI that lets us start the Apache web server. But in Linux we need to enter the following command as a root user.

root @ kali: service apache start

This will start the web server in the background, which can be accessed from the localhost. You can check if everything is going well or not using ps command.

Step 2: Accessing the local host

Now after starting the server you can go to your local host address that is http://127.0.0.1 using your browser to access apache. You will be welcomed with an apache page that asks your permission to show the default page.

Step 3: Modify the webpage

Now for a practical example, modify html file to your desired and save it using any text editor. After few seconds come back to localhost and refresh. Boom! You can see the modified webpage. This confirms that service is being run on the background.

How an apache web server can help hackers?

Programmers to create a local host website during development phase usually use Apache web server. This can be linked with WAMP to further expand it with Php or MySQL servers. However, hackers can use it to learn about loopholes in websites without being blocked or banned. Hackers can also use Apache web server applications like Vulnerable App to expand their hacking skills. Almost every Hackathon program use the Apache web server for making their Hacking boxes.

Logging system

Being a hacker, you will certainly visit networks with high-level protection and maintained by hardworking security engineers. And if with all your skills you have exploited the system. After the attack, obviously a forensic investigation will take place and will try to find how an attack has been planned and executed. Everything of this investigation will be based on logfiles that you have left while exploiting the system.

Linux unlike windows is not vulnerable to exploits and attacking's because it has good logging system that records everything the user does. But some smart hackers use different techniques to make themselves undetectable by reading logfiles. We will explain in detail about how hackers need to develop skills to manipulate the logging system.

rsyslog

rsyslog is a definite daemon program that takes care of log files to be created in the UNIX or Linux system. Every Linux distribution uses different techniques to deploy log files. Arch Linux uses a different process unlike Debian rsyslog function. As we are discussing about kali Linux that is a Debian system we will continue with rsyslog explanation along with few examples.

kern.*   -var/log/kern.log

This is where log instructions are given to the Linux kernel. When we look at it thoroughly, we will find a basic command that log functionality uses. It is as the command shown below.

facility.priority action

We need to describe these three things in detail to get a thorough overview about the concept.

1) Facility

Facility is something, which is being logged. For example, mail designates about the mail system. There are few that comes under this category as explained below.

a) mail

This explains about the mailing system that is present in kali Linux. This precisely says that mail usage is being logged

b) user

All user related instructions or functions comes under this category.

c) kern

All messages that deals with the kernel comes under this category

d) lpr

All messages that deals with the inbuilt printing system comes under this.

2) Priority

If the facility describes which messages to log, priority decides on what to log. There are different types of messages that can be used to a better logging system. We will describe some of them below.

a) debug

This is used to log the things that happen as it is.

b) warning

This is used to log things that work but can go wrong.

c) info

This is used to log about normal information that exists. This can also be used to log date and time.

d) error

This can be used if something badly goes wrong while doing a work in Linux.

3) Action

This is quite simple to understand than the rest. It just means that the logs should be sent into this particular category. We may manually assign folder but it's better to leave them, as it is to go to var folder for better management. We will give some example destinations that logs are sent normally

a) Kernel files:

These are normally sent to /var/log/kernel . You can just go to the directory and open the log file using leafpad to analyze them.

Now as we have learned everything we will just look at an example that deals with all of this.

mail.warning /var/log/warning

This precisely means that mail system warning message logs will be sent to /var/log/warning path.

Automatically clean logs

Log files can make up a lot of mess if you use them extensively. We need to make a strategy to keep how many logs depending on the time interval. However, we can use logrotate function in kali Linux to configure few functions that can help us clean log files.

Open logrotate.conf file and modify the text file to create your own log system according to your own necessity.

How to spoof log files?

You might wonder being a hacker how people get rid of tracking when they attack any target host. Luckily, Linux provides few functions, which can help us to spoof log files that is to modify them in a way such that network administrators cannot detect what happened during the attack. This process is called shred. We will explain about this process in detail in the below section.

Step 1:

Shred function just fills the log data with randomly generated UTF-8 code in the logged data again and again to make it as unusable data. To check shred function just click the below command in the Linux terminal as a root user.

root @ kali: shred

Step 2:
To make any file into unusable shred file you need to call the shred command with the file name. That's it. With a single click, all your data will be made into a difficult data that cannot be read or understood by anyone. The command is as below:

root @ kali: shred (insert file name here)

root @ kali: shred desktop/kalishred.txt

Step 3:
There is a special function in shred command that can help you shred the file as number of times you needed to be. But the only negative thing to worry about this is when you try to shred a file by 20 times the time taken will increase exponentially. So always listen to your senses when trying to shred a file multiple times. -n command describes the number of times function. Command is shown as below:

root @ kali : shred -n 20 /desktop/kalishred.txt

There is also another way to make logging stop. When you have control over system as a root user, you can simply disable the service by using the following command. We can use three commands start, stop and restart for this service.

a) start

This starts the logging function allover again.

root@kali: service rsyslog start

b) stop

This stops the logging function in a split of a second.

root@kali: service rsyslog stop

c) Restart

This will first stop the logging function and will start again as a new variable.

root@kali: service rsyslog restart

Automating tasks with job scheduling

As a hacker, the most important skill you need to learn is to automate things. Whenever you attack a system or exploit a system, you need to get ready with a ton of things that will automate things for you. An automated backup or automated deletion of logfiles everything needs to be done for a better productivity and results. In this section, we will discuss in detail about automating tasks using kali Linux.

crontab

Crontab is a function that is available in kali Linux that will let us schedule an event or job for a particular time. We can enter the data from minutes to years to start a crontab task.

root @ kali : crontab

Click -help to check the functions of the crontab in detail.

Scheduling a backup task

Backup is one of the essential thing to do whenever you are dealing with an important data. When data is backed up, it can be used as an alternative if there is any leakage or corrupt in data. So administrators always prefer backing up the data. But it is a difficult and boring task to backup manually every day. So we can create an automatic backup with the following command.

00 1 18,28 ** backup/desktop/backup.sh

Here first 00 stands for the top of the hour. And ** to any day of the month.

Crontab shortcuts

Below we will display a few shortcuts that are used in crontab automatic task scheduling.

1) @yearly

This will make the task to run once a year.

2) @ weekly

This will make a task to run once in a week

3) @ midnight

This will make a task to run at midnight every day.

Starting tasks at startup with rc

While startup certain scripts start their tasks automatically using rc scripts. This will help them prioritize in the process and will give good results. If you are willing to add a service to start automatically on a startup, you can use the following command.

root @ kali : update-
rc.d servicename enable/disable

Protecting you with TOR and VPN

It is obvious that the most important thing for any hacker is his anonymity. Now days due to restrictions of Government and constant spying had made people to find alternate options to maintain anonymity like TOR and VPN. Before going to learn how to maintain your anonymity in Kali Linux, we will have a good explanation about all the options we have for securing ourselves in this matrix world that is all connected.

Why Anonymity matters?
Imagine if your country has blocked your internet access to social networking during riots and all of your people want to use it for better communication. You can do with a VPN or TOR bundle and not are detected. However, tracking can be done in any other way if they want to. But make sure to follow this for some better peace. In the below section we will learn about anonymity services that has different uses.

What is a proxy server?

Proxy is a middle man between you and server that you are trying to reach. Imagine if you want to deliver a package from New York (your place) to Colorado (Server place). Instead of going and giving the package all by your own, you will ask your friend to deliver it. Here your friend acts a proxy for you. This is how the proxy server works.

There are many proxy servers like Socks4, http, https and Socks5.

How a hacker can use proxy server?

When doing a password attack you will normally be blocked by the website due to too many requests. In these situations, you can use a bunch of free proxies to randomly occupy the proxy address and attack the login page. This is a famous technique called cracking that Is used by novice hackers to get an access into the system.

What is a VPN?

A VPN is a quite common advertisement that you might have used while watching ads in YouTube. A virtual private network abbreviated as a VPN acts like a middle man but delivers your request in encrypted form to the server in such a way that the server can't identify you. And when the server sends you the response it again encrypts it and sends towards you. Imagine this example to get a better understanding of how a Vpn works. Imagine that you want to deliver a Love Letter to your classmate. But you don't want any other person to read it other than your best friend. So, you write a Letter in quite a different way that no one can understand and sends by your friend to your classmate. Remember that your friends know how to read it. He will decrypt it to her and she will send a response in the same way. This is basically how a VPN works.

In the next section, we will describe about how internet communication works and will give a practical example that will let us understand the fact that Anonymity is a must.

How the internet works?

Every internet connected device has an IP address that can be easily tracked using different techniques by the government. When u send an email or surf internet without any Anonymity services, you are just being a product to Tech giants like Google. They will collect a lot of information from you and will sell you as adds to the businesses. Apart from that, every movement of yours will be tracked and can help them create new products.

Normally when we click on an URL the packet that contains your request will also contain the IP addresses of both yours and the server that you are trying to reach. In the communication process, it will travel through different routers called hops before reaching its final destination. When a packet is travelling, it can be easily sniffed and can be used to acquire information about you.

For an example, use traceroute command to check how many hops that a particular website takes as below.

root @ kali: traceroute bing.com

You will get an output that shows the number of routers it needs to travel to reach the final destination. When the packet is travelling, anyone can sniff it and can attain sensitive information about you and your request.

Chapter 5 Bash Scripting and Python Scripting

What is bash Scripting? A shell script is basically a text file that contains containing a string of commands in sequence. When the script is run, it executes all the commands that are in the file. The "shell" in the phrase refers to the command-line user interface that is used to communicate with the Linux kernel. There are a few different shells currently in use, with the most common ones being the C shell or csh, the Korn shell or ksh, the Bourne shell or sh, and the Bourne-Again shell or bash.

There are a number of scenarios that will require you to script with the shell. You may for instance have to support existing scripts, or you may wish to automate the system setup procedure before installing Oracle. In this scenario, you may use a script to determine the state of the operating system and any system requirements that you will have to meet before the software can be installed.

Linux

The most commonly used shell under Linux is called "Bash". This name is derived from "Bourne Again Shell". Although there are many other types of shells available for Linux, most experts recommend that you stick to the Bash shell, since this will increase the portability of your scripts between different systems and operating systems.

UNIX

Under UNIX, the shell allows a programmer to string together and execute a number of UNIX commands without having to compile them first. This makes it a lot faster to get a script running. In addition, shell scripting under UNIX makes it easier for other programmers to read and understand your code. Such shell scripts are also usually easily portable across the entire UNIX world, as long as they conform to a set standard.

Scripting for Windows

The Windows operating system conveniently includes a basic command structure that can be used to create scripts that will essentially streamline various administrative tasks. Some of the more common scripting languages under the Windows platform are Windows shell scripting, Visual Basic Scripting or VBS, and JScript. Shell scripting on the Windows platform is commonly used to produce logon scripts, which are in turn used to configure the Windows environment for specific uses when they log on. Marketing personnel for instance may use such scripts to automatically map network drives to the marketing network folder, and so on.

Despite what assembly code and C coders might tell us, high-level languages do have their place in every programmer's toolbox, and some of them are much more than a computer-science curiosity. Out of the many high-level languages we can choose from today, Python seems to be the most interesting for those who want to learn something new and do real work at the same time. Its no-nonsense implementation of object-oriented programming and its clean and easy-to-understand syntax make it a language that is fun to learn and use, which is not something we can say about most other languages.

In Python Training, you will learn how to write applications that use command-line options, read and write to pipes, access environment variables, handle interrupts, read from and write to files, create temporary files and write to system logs. In other words, you will find recipes for writing real applications instead of the old boring Hello, World! stuff.

Getting Started

To begin, if you have not installed the Python interpreter on your system, now is the time. To make that step easier, install the latest Python distribution using packages compatible with your Linux distribution. rpm, deb and tgz are also available on your Linux CD-ROM or on-line. If you follow standard installation procedures, you should not have any problems.

I also recommend that you have the Python Library Reference handy; you might want it when the explanations given here do not meet your needs. You can find it in the same places as the Python Tutorial.

Creating scripts can be done using your favorite text editor as long as it saves text in plain ASCII format and does not automatically insert line breaks when the line is longer than the width of the editor's window.

Always begin your scripts with either

#! /usr/local/bin/python

or

```
#! /usr/bin/python
```

If the access path to the python binary on your system is different, change that line, leaving the first two characters (#!) intact. Be sure this line is truly the first line in your script, not just the first non-blank line-it will save you a lot of frustration.

Use chmod to set the file permissions on your script to make it executable. If the script is for you alone, type chmod 0700 scriptfilename.py; if you want to share it with others in your group but not let them edit it, use 0750 as the chmod value; if you want to give access to everyone else, use the value 0755. For help with the chmod command, type man chmod.

Reading Command-Line Options and Arguments

Command-line options and arguments come in handy when we want to tell our scripts how to behave or pass some arguments (file names, directory names, user names, etc.) to them. All programs can read these options and arguments if they want, and your Python scripts are no different.

Bash script can be utilized for different purposes, for example, executing a shell order, running various directions together, tweaking managerial errands, performing task robotization and so on. So information of slam programming nuts and bolts is significant for each Linux client. This section will assist you with getting the fundamental thought on slam programming. A large portion of the regular activities of slam scripting are clarified with extremely basic models here.

Bash script can be utilized for different purposes, for example, executing a shell direction, running various directions together, modifying managerial errands, performing task robotization and so on. So learning of slam programming nuts and bolts is significant for each Linux client. This part will assist you with getting the essential thought on slam programming.

A typical example of bash scripting is sh-bang #!/bin/bash -e and an example of python scripting is magic 8-ball and port scanner in phyth

Chapter 6 Wireless Hacking

The proliferation of readily available Wi-Fi networks has made Wi-Fi one of the most common network mediums. Wi-Fi is in many ways superior to traditional copper wire physically connected networks. Aside from the convenience of connectivity and the flexibility of network configurations that wireless networks afford the users, the lack of physical infrastructure needed to complete the network makes it much cheaper and easier to implement than Ethernet. With this convenience, however, comes certain security concerns that are not associated with traditional hardwired networks. With a copper or fiber-based network, a physical connection is needed for a new machine to join the network. A hacker would normally have difficulty accessing the physical space of a target network and would likely arouse suspicion attempting to connect their own hardware to network cabling. Although the range of Wi-Fi is limited, it is omnidirectional and the radiofrequency signals admitted by the server and the various nodes on a wireless network traverse walls and other barriers and can be intercepted by anyone in range. This gives the hacker much more freedom to conduct a network intrusion without being detected.

Hacking Wi-Fi

Most Wi-Fi networks consist of a wireless router, or a group of wireless routers, that are connected to a modem which is delivering internet access to some physical location. The routers broadcast and receive radio signals on specific channels that carry the appropriate TCP/IP packets to and from other machines and devices that have similar wireless connectivity. All nodes communicating at any given time on the channels associated with the router or routers that are connected to the modem at that location comprise a Wi-Fi network. By nature, Wi-Fi networks are very dynamic and fluid. Especially in commercial settings, like coffee shops or office buildings that provide wireless access, the number and nature of the nodes on that particular network are in constant flux. In these public settings, it is easy for a hacker to hide in plain sight and attempt to intrude into any of the nodes on the network. Once the hacker is successfully on the network itself, they can scan the network for all connected machines and probe for vulnerabilities. Many networks have both wireless and wired subnetworks that are interconnected. When a hacker gains access to a wireless network they can conceivably use that to leverage access to all of the nodes on the wired portion of the network. This makes Wi-Fi hacking a very popular goal for modern hackers.

Wi-Fi Encryption Protocols

Since Wi-Fi signals are broadcast into the air as opposed to being confined within wires, it is important for the information contained in the signals to be encrypted. Otherwise, anyone could passively receive and view any information being sent between the nodes on the network. The encryption protocols used in Wi-Fi have necessarily evolved since wireless networks began gaining popularity. Moreover, as technology has improved and resulted in increased bandwidth and data rates, a great density of information can be broadcast from a wireless network in a very short period of time, making it especially important for it to be encrypted and kept out of the hands of malicious hackers.

The oldest and most common Wi-Fi encryption protocol is Wired Equivalent Privacy (WEP). The goal of the WEP standard, as the name implies, was to give network users the same amount of security that they would have on a physically connected network. Unfortunately, over time WEP has become the least secure of all of the existing encryption protocols and it is quite easily hacked by even the most inexperienced hackers. WEP is so insecure in fact, that many Wi-Fi router manufacturers no longer provide that type of encryption as an option on their hardware. Most security professionals recommend that router owners do not use WEP when other options are available. Step-by-step instructions and coding examples for attacking WEP protected Wi-Fi networks are freely and readily available on the internet. Although the level of encryption has increased from 64 bit to 128 bit to 256 bit, the underlying flaws in WEP remain easily exploitable by even the most green of neophyte hackers. The biggest problem with WEP is that a password can be quickly and easily deciphered simply through the passive "sniffing" (receiving and viewing network packets) of network traffic.

A significant step up from WEP Wi-Fi encryption is the Wi-Fi Protected Access (WPA) standard of encryption. This new protocol fixed many of the problems in WEP, but remained vulnerable to attack because it was still based on some of the same underlying encryption algorithms. Furthermore, WPA-protected routers were deployed with a feature that was designed to make it more convenient for home users to connect new devices to their network. This feature proved to be an additional vulnerability in systems that employed WPA.

It wasn't long before an update to WPA was needed to keep Wi-Fi networks more secure. A new encryption standard being used in other secure applications, the Advanced Encryption Standard (AES), became mandatory in the new Wi-Fi encryption protocol which became known as WPA-2. WPA-2 with AES encryption has become the recommended setting for wireless routers on which it is available because of its significant improvement

in security over its preceding standards. Cracking WPA and WPA-2 requires more intrusive hacking techniques than the simple passive sniffing that can be used to attack WEP-protected networks.

Wi-Fi Attacks

In order to conduct a Wi-Fi attack a hacker needs, at a minimum, a computer (normally a laptop) that can run scripts which are used to decipher the Wi-Fi password. They also must acquire a special Wi-Fi adapter that can be purchased relatively cheaply. A list of suitable Wi-Fi adapters can be found on hacker resource websites, but in general the adapter must have a feature known as "monitor mode" in order to be able to execute a Wi-Fi attack. It is important to note that not all Wi-Fi adapters that can be found at retail computer supply stores have this feature, and most internal laptop adapters are not appropriate. In general, hackers prefer to use some sort of Linux distribution, usually Kali, to conduct a Wi-Fi attack because most of the readily available tools were written for the Linux OS and come preinstalled on Kali. It is also possible with some configuration to run Linux on a virtual machine within another OS to mount a successful attack. Although attacks from other operating systems are possible, it is much easier for the beginner to conduct them from either a native Linux distribution or a virtual machine. A hacker-friendly distribution like Kali is recommended.

The detailed procedures and recommended programs for conducting Wi-Fi attacks against the various encryption protocols changes over time, although the general principles are the same. For the simplest attack, which is against WEP encryption, the general steps are as follows:

1) monitor and view all Wi-Fi traffic in the range of the adapter while in "monitor mode" (set by a program called *airmon-ng*) using a program called *airodump-ng.*

Live W-Fi Traffic on Several Routers (aircrack-ng.org)

2) choose a target Wi-Fi network that is using WEP encryption and make a note of the name (ESSID) and network address (BSSID in the form XX:XX:XX:XX:XX:XX)
3) restart *airodump-ng* to begin capturing network traffic from the specific network that you are targeting
4) wait for a sufficient number of packets to be captured (this may take longer on networks with less traffic)

5) use a program called *aircrack-ng* to piece together the captured network packets into a coherent password

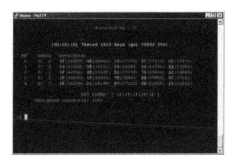

A Successfully Decrypted Wi-Fi Key (<u>aircrack-ng.org</u>)

If network traffic is too slow to capture a sufficient number of packets for decrypting the password in a reasonable period of time, some hackers choose to use a program called *aireplay-ng* to inject artificial packets into the network and create the necessary traffic to crack it more quickly. However, this activity requires the hacker's machine to actually broadcast signals from its Wi-Fi adapter, making it more conspicuous.

WPA encryption cannot be cracked passively and requires the additional step of packet injection. Cracking WPA can

take longer and is a more invasive procedure, but it is not much more difficult than cracking WEP. A program called *reaver*, normally available on the Kali distribution is typically used by hackers to crack

WPA. WPA-2 hacking is a much more advanced concept for more experienced practitioners. (Note: the software tools above are pre-installed on Kali Linux, or can be downloaded from www.aircrack-ng.org)

Chapter 7 Your First Hack

The neophyte hacker shouldn't even think about attempting an attack on a real target as their first foray into hacking. Sufficient tools and technologies exist which are easily obtained and with which various methods can be rehearsed in a virtual environment. This type of practice is essential for the hacker and is more valuable than all of the reading and study one could accomplish. To build confidence and gain appreciation for the nuances and practical pitfalls, the beginning hacker should aspire to accomplish the simple attacks suggested in this chapter. The details of the attacks will vary and currently applicable instructions should be researched by the reader, but the general principles of the setup and execution should be fairly universal.

Hacking Your Own Wi-Fi

The purpose of this practice attack is to successfully obtain the password of a WEP-encrypted Wi-Fi network. To minimize risk, the network and any connected devices should be owned or controlled by you, or by someone who has given you explicit permission to perform penetration testing.

What you need:

1) A computer
2) A wireless network adapter that supports "monitor mode"
3) Access to a Wi-Fi router with WEP encryption (does not have to have internet access)
4) The latest version of Kali Linux (installed as the primary OS or in a virtual machine)

Setting up:

1) Ensure that the router is set to WEP and give it a password of your choice
2) Turn off the internal Wi-Fi adapter on your laptop if you have one
3) Connect the "monitor mode" adapter to your attack machine and install any necessary drivers
4) Be sure the attack computer is in wireless range of the target network

Procedure:

1) Follow the "Wi-Fi Hacking" steps
2) Confirm that the cracked password matches the one you set for the network
3) Repeat the hack using aireplay-ng for packet injection and compare execution times
4) Change the length or complexity of the password and repeat the hack, comparing execution times

A Virtual Windows Vulnerability Assessment
Operating systems contain multiple software vulnerabilities that hackers are ready and willing to exploit. When a hacker discovers an un-patched version of an OS, there are a number of commonly available exploits with which to gain access. The first step in deploying those exploits is to analyze the OS for the most glaring vulnerabilities. Kali Linux features natively installed tools that will scan a system and provide a list of vulnerabilities. This exercise will require two virtual machines running within the same system (regardless of the host OS). It will also require an installation image for an older, unsupported, and un-patched version of Microsoft Windows (Windows '95 or '98 are good choices). These images can be obtained online (usgcb.nist.gov) or from an old CD.

What you need:

1) A computer with any OS
2) Virtualization software
3) The latest version of Kali Linux
4) An unsupported, un-patched version of Microsoft Windows

Setting up:

1) Install Kali Linux on a virtual machine
2) Install the target Windows distribution on a virtual machine (on the same host system as Kali)

Procedure:

1) Execute a network scan from the Kali virtual machine using a program called *nmap*
2) Practice changing various settings in *nmap* so that OS vulnerabilities will be detected and displayed
3) Make note of the listed Windows vulnerabilities and begin researching exploits!

Chapter 8 Scanning Ports

The reason you are going to want to scan ports is so that you can find an open one. With ports, you are going to be able to get into someone's system and leave a door open so that you can get in again later on. Port scans use host scans which can take up a lot of time if you have a wide range of IP addresses that have to be scanned and most of them end up being vacant.

Ports That Are Open

A network scanner is going to be used when you are connected to either of these ports and as soon as the port accepts the connection from the scanner, it is going to be best for you to assume that the program that is bound is running as it should be.

TCP ports are going to work with SYN packets that are sent back and forth between the servers, and the clients use them. Whenever the packet is sent to the server, it is going to send a SYN/ACK packet back resulting in the client sending the ACK packet back. After the SYN packet is received once more by the client, the port is going to be opened. In the off chance that an RST packet is sent instead, then the port is going to be closed. If the server does not send anything, then there is probably a firewall that is blocking it from the port or the port is not running on that IP address.

When you are scanning UDP ports, you are going to most likely run into problems because there are no handshakes exchanged and the programs are going to get rid of any packets that they are not going to be able to process. UDP packets are going to be sent to a port without a program that is bound to it. ICMP error packets are going to be what is returned. From there you are most likely going to consider the port to be closed. No answer is going to mean that a firewall is filtering out the packets or the port is opened. Too many people end up leaving their UDP scans because these scanners have difficulty telling the difference between when a port is opened and when it is filtering the packets.

Ports That Are More Common

To save yourself some time, Nmap is going to scan around 1667 ports that are going to be the default ports. But, you are going to get more results if you thoroughly scan all the ports; and there are 65536 ports. So, if you have the time, scan them all!

Port Specifications

When you are using the -p command, you are going to be able to tell the Nmap program exactly which ports you want it to scan so that you can save time on your scanning.

Target Specifications

Just like you can tell Nmap to scan specific ports, you can also tell it to go after a specific host or set of hosts. This host is going to be verified only by putting in the IP address for that host or by using the domain name. Should you wish to scan several different ports, you are going to want to set up the range for the IP addresses.

Scan Types

TCP SYN

A TCP SYN scan is going to be the default scan done by Nmap. When you use the -sS command, the program will only do that scan. As the administrator, you are going to be allowed to start the scan. If a user starts the scan, then a connect scan is going to be performed.

TCP connect

There is a command that you can use to make sure that Nmap has a full connection and that is the -sT command. This scan is not going to be as good as the TCP SYN scan because there is more that has to be sent back and forth between the client and the server. This scan is going to be executed with user privileges or whenever an IPv6 address is being scanned.

TCP null

When you use the -sN option, the program is going to send back all packets that do not have anything to do with SYN, ACK, or RST flags. If it comes back that the port is closed, the RST packet is going to be the one returned. If the port is opened or has a firewall filtering its packets, then there is not going to be a response sent back. Doing a null scan is going to be the best way to attempt to get passed the stateless firewall however if the firewall is stateful then it is not going to do anything.

UDP empty packet

When you use the -sU function, Nmap is going to send out UDP packets that contain no data. If an error message is returned, then you are going to assume that the port is closed. However, when there is no response, you will assume the port is opened or filtered. This scan cannot tell the difference between a filtered port or an open port which is going to leave some severe limitation in your scan.

UDP application

You are going to use -SU or -SV options to tell the program that you want data from an application or for the application to be identified. Since this has several different options put together, you are going to experience a slow scan.

Scanning Speed

Like most things, if things are sent at a speed that is faster than the system can deal with, then the packets are going to be dropped, and they are not going to be used in the scan thus you are going to get results that are not accurate. If there is an intrusion detection or an intrusion prevention that is in place on the target's network, then the faster that the scan is going through, the more likely that it is that you are going to be detected by the target.

There are a lot of devices as well as firewalls that work with IPS that are meant to respond to SYN packets that are sent in from the cookies created by these packets so that every port appears open even if they are not. When you are running a scan at full speed, then you are going to risk wreaking havoc on the network devices that are stateful.

With Nmap, there will be five templates that you can use to adjust the speed in case it does not adjust itself properly. With the -T0 option, you are going to force the program to wait about five minutes in between sending packets. -T1 waits for fifteen seconds, -T2 for 0.4 seconds, and -T3 which is going to be the default setting where the timing goes unchanged. Lastly, when -T4 is used, the timeouts are reduced, but the retransmission speed is upped ever so slightly. -T5 is similar to -T4but things are going to be sped up even more. A modern IPS or IDS device is going to figure out the scans that are using -T1 and detect that device so that the hacker is discovered. As the user of Nmap, you can also decide to make a new template with new parameters if you are not happy with the ones that are provided.

Identifying Applications

If you decide to use the -SV option, then Nmap is going to have to figure out which version of the application is currently being run.

Identifying the Operating System

If you want to discover which operating system is being used by the target, you will use the -O option in Nmap. There are packets that are specially crafted to be sent to the target to all of the ports so that the responses can be analyzed in the database that you are using on your operating system.

Save

When you want to save the output that you get returned to you, you will use the -oX<filename> option so that it is saved in an XML format.

Chapter 9 Attacking With Frameworks

Social Engineering

Due to the increase in the use of technology for almost all of our activities, companies and organizations have invested a huge amount of money in ensuring that the technologies they use are properly secured from hackers. These companies have developed and implemented extensive firewalls to protect against any possible security breach. Most internet users are not security conscious despite the ease with which information can be obtained over an internet connection. This is coupled with the fact that most malicious hackers concentrate their efforts on computer servers and client application flaws. Over the years, these hackers have become more creative in how they gather information and structure their attacks on websites and web apps. With the enormous amount of money invested in online security, we would expect that malicious information theft or control would have been eliminated. However, this has not happened.

This is where we use social engineering to achieve our goal. It is a non-technical approach circumvents a company's security measures. No matter how secure a company's online applications are, they are still susceptible to hacking. Hackers have been able to achieve this using social engineering and tools based on social engineering. Social engineering is a hands-on approach to hacking. It involves targeting individuals and manipulating them into giving out vital information that can lead to a breach in the security system. These individuals, who may be employees of the organization or even a close relative of the top person at the target organization, are approached and coerced into trusting the hacker. They begin to gather information that could be of use in the hacking process. This is usually an approach taken when the company's firewalls are effective at thwarting outside penetration. When the hackers have obtained the necessary information (for instance, the login information of the social engineering target), they can hack the company from the inside out.

It is believed that human beings are the weakest link in any information security chain. The physical approach toward social engineering can occur in so many ways that it is impossible to cover all of them in this chapter. However, popular means include approaching and becoming friends with (or even a significant other of) employees at the company. Sometimes the employees are given a flash drive containing movies or other files in which they may be interested. The employees plug in the drive and launch a file that executes scripts in the background, granting the hackers access to the respective machines. The social engineer attack can also occur when a person calls an employee of a firm, impersonates a call center representative and tells the employee that he or she needs information to rectify a service that is important. The hacker would have gathered details about the employee from the employee's social media account or through personal conversations with the person. Once the hacker has received the information (which may include the victim's social security number or login details), the hacker hijacks the account and performs fraudulent transactions on it, or uses it for additional attacks. Social engineering makes it easy to build a username and password list that helps with logging into the target's accounts.

Hackers use the information they have gathered in combination with tools that ensure an easy hack of the company's system. Most of these tools are used in the client-side attack and are enhanced with the information gathered through social engineering. This information is used in conjunction with phishing and spoofing tools to attack a client if a direct social engineering attack fails. Social engineering is the information gathering procedure in this approach when it comes to attacking clients. Hacking has become a business venture. Hackers gain access to information simply to sell it for money, or to use it to transfer money. The motivation now is monetary. Usually, the target is selected, and the hacker uses information available to the public about the client to develop the attack. Typically, information obtained online is sufficient to build an attack. However, with an increase in employee education regarding hackers and social engineering, employees have begun to limit the personal information they share on social media and other public platforms.

The success of a social-engineering-based attack depends solely on the quality of information gathered. The attacker must be sociable and persuasive when interacting with the victim, such that the victim becomes open and begins to trust the hacker. Some hackers outsource this aspect to an individual who is skilled in getting people to tell them secrets.

Social Engineering Toolkit (SET)

The Social Engineering Toolkit is a very important tool used in a computer-aided social engineering attack. It comes pre-installed with the Kali Linux distro. It is written in the Python language and is also an open source toolkit. The Social Engineering Toolkit, or SET, was created by David Kennedy to exploit the human aspect of web security. However, it is important to make sure that the Social Engineering Toolkit is up to date. Once the tool has been updated, the configuration file can be set. The default configuration file is sufficient to make the SET run without any problems. Advanced users may want to edit and tweak certain settings. However, if you are a beginner, it is better to leave it the way it is until you become more familiar with the Social Engineering Toolkit. To access the configuration file, open the terminal and then change the directory to the SET. Open the config folder and you will find the set_config file, which you can open and edit with a text editor to change the parameters.

The Social Engineering Toolkit can be accessed by clicking on the Application icon, then clicking on the Kali Linux desktop. Next, click on BackTrack and then on the Exploitation Tools option. Click on Social Engineering Tools and select the Social Engineering Toolkit by clicking on SET. The SET will open in a terminal window. Alternatively, the SET can be opened directly from the terminal by typing "setoolkit" without the quotes.

The Social Engineering Toolkit opens in the terminal as a menu-based option. The menu contains different options based on the type of social engineering attack you need to use. The option at number 1 is for spear-phishing vectors which enable the user to execute a phishing attack. The phishing attack is an email attack. It is like casting a net by sending emails to random potential victims. Spear-phishing, on the other hand, targets one individual and the email is more personalized.

The second option on the SET menu is the website attack vector, which uses different web-attack methods against its target victim. The website attack vector option is by far the most popular and perhaps most used option in the Social Engineering Toolkit. Clicking on the website attack vector option opens menus containing the Java applet attack vector, the Metasploit browser exploits, the credential harvester attack used in cloning websites, the tabnabbing attack, the man-in-the-middle attack, the web jacking attack and the multi-attack web method.

The third option on the Social Engineering Toolkit menu is the infectious media generator tool. This is a very easy tool to use and is targeted at individuals who can give a hacker access to the organization network, thus enabling the hacker to hack from inside the network. This tool allows the hacker to create a USB disk or DVD containing a malicious script that gives the hacker access to the target shell. Choosing this option opens a menu with a prompt to choose from between a file-format exploit or a standard Metasploit executable. Choosing the file-format option opens a list of payloads from which to select. The default is a PDF file embedded in an executable script. This is then sent to the drive where the autorun.inf is created with the PDF file. When an employee opens the file on the drive, the file is executed in the background and the hacker gains shell access to the victim's computer.

The fourth option is the generate-a-payload-with-listener option. This option allows the hacker to create a malicious script as a payload and therefore generate a listener. This script is a .exe file. The key is getting the intended victim to click and download this script. Once the victim downloads the .exe file and executes it, the listener alerts the hacker, who can access the victim's shell.

The fifth option in the Social Engineering Toolkit is the mass mailer option. Clicking this option brings up a menu with two options: single email address attack and the mass mailer email attack. The single email address attack allows the user to send an email to a single email address while the mass mailer email attack allows the user to send an email to multiple email addresses. Choosing this option prompts the user to select a list containing multiple email addresses to which the email is then sent.

Sixth on the list is the Arduino-based attack. With this option, you are given the means to compromise Arduino-based devices. The seventh option, on the other hand, is the SMS spoofing option, which enables the hacker to send SMS to a person. This SMS spoofing option opens a menu with an option to perform an SMS spoofing form of attack or create a social-engineering template. Selecting the first option will send to a single number or a mass SMS attack. Selecting just a single number prompts the user to enter the recipient's phone number. Then you are asked to either use a predefined template or craft your own message. Typing 1 chooses the first option while typing 2 chooses the second option depending on your preference for the SMS. Then you enter the source number, which is the number you want the recipient to see as the sender of the SMS. Next, you type the message you want the recipient to see. You can embed links to a phishing site or to a page that will cause the user to download a malicious .exe file. After the message has been crafted, the options for services used in SMS spoofing appear on the screen. Some are paid options and others are free.

Option eight in the SET is the wireless AP attack vector. This option is used to create a fake wireless AP to which unsuspecting users of public Wi-Fi can connect and the hacker can sniff their traffic. This option uses other applications in achieving this goal. AirBase-NG, AirMon-NG, DNSSpoof and dhcpd3 are the required applications that work hand in hand with the wireless AP attack vector.

Option nine in the menu is the QR code attack vector. Today, QR codes are used everywhere, from the identification of items to obtaining more details about products on sale. Now QR codes are even used to make payments. Some websites use QR codes for logins or as web apps. This login method is used because it is perceived as a more secure way of gaining access due to hackers' being able to steal cookies, execute a man-in-the-middle attack and even use a brute-force password to gain unauthorized access. However, this increase in the use of QR codes has given hackers more avenues for exploiting their victims. The QR code attack vector helps the hacker create a malicious QR code. Then the hacker creates or clones a website like Facebook using the credential harvester option and embeds this malicious QR code with the link to the cloned website. The hacker then sends a phishing email or spoofed SMS to a victim, which prompts that person to scan the code with a mobile device. This reveal's the victim's GPS location and other information when the victim visits the website and enters their login details.

The tenth option in the menu is the PowerShell attack vector. This option allows the hacker to deploy payloads in the PowerShell of an operating system. The PowerShell is a more powerful option than the command prompt in the Windows operating system. It allows access to different areas of the operating system. It was developed by Microsoft to ease the automation of tasks and configuration of files and has come with the Windows operating system since the release of Windows Vista. The PowerShell attack vector enables the attacker to create a script that is then executed in the victim's PowerShell. The selection of this option brings out four menu options: PowerShell alphanumeric injector, PowerShell SAM database, PowerShell reverse and PowerShell bind shells. Any of these options creates a targeted PowerShell program and is exported to the PowerShell folder. Tricking the target to access, download and execute this program creates access for the attacker.

By now, you should realize how powerful the SET is in executing computer-aided social engineering attacks. This tool is very valuable for a penetration tester, as it provides a robust and diverse means of checking the various vulnerabilities that may exist in an organization's network.

BeEF

BeEF stands for Browser Exploitation Framework. This tool comes with most of the security-based Linux distro, like the Parrot OS and Kali Linux. BeEF started as a server that was accessed through the attacker's browser. It was created to target vulnerabilities in web browsers that would give access to the target systems for executing commands. BeEF was written in the Ruby language on the Rails platform by a team headed by Wade Alcorn. As stated before, passwords, cookies, login credentials and browsing history are all typically stored on the browser, so a BeEF attack on a client can be very nasty.

On Kali Linux, however, BeEF has been included in the distro. The BeEF framework can be started by going into applications, clicking on exploitation tools and then clicking on the BeEF XSS framework. This brings up a terminal that shows the BeEF framework server has been started. Once the server has been started, we open our browser of choice and visit the localhost at port 3000. This is written in the URL space of the browser as localhost:3000/ui/authentication or 127.0.0.1:3000/ui/authentication. This would bring us to the authentication page of the BeEF framework, requiring a login username and password. By default, the username is beef ; the password is also beef.

Once you are in the BeEF framework, it will open a "Get Started" tab. Here you are introduced to the framework and learn how to use it. Of particular importance is hooking a browser. Hooking a browser involves clicking a JavaScript payload that gives the BeEF framework access to the client's browser. There are various ways by which we can deploy this payload, but the simplest way is to create a page with the payload, prompt the target to visit that page and execute the JavaScript payload. You can be very creative about this aspect. On the other hand, there is a link on the Get Started page that redirects you to The Butcher page. Below this page are buttons containing the JavaScript payload. Clicking on this button will execute the script and, in turn, hook your browser. When your browser is hooked, you will see a hook icon beside your browser icon on the left side of the BeEF control panel with the title "Hooked browser" along with folders for online and offline browsers.

Once a browser is hooked, whether it's online or offline, we can control it from our BeEF control panel. Clicking on the details menu in the control panel will provide information like the victim's browser version and the plugins that are installed. The window size of the browser also can be used to determine the victim's screen size, the browser platform (which is also the operating system on the PC), and a lot more information. For executing commands on the browser, we click on the command menu in the control panel. This brings up a different command we can execute on the victim's browser. This command would create a pop-up message on the victim's browser, so it can be renamed creatively before execution to avoid raising any suspicion. Some of the commands that can be executed in this menu include the Get all Cookie command (which starts harvesting the victim's browser cookies), the Screenshot command, the Webcam command for taking pictures of the victim, the Get visited URL command and so on. There are a lot of commands in this menu.

The BeEF framework JavaScript payload can also hook mobile phone browsers. Checking the details tab after hooking will give that particular information if we end up hooking a phone browser. Clicking on the module and searching the PhoneGap command allows us to execute phone targeted commands like geolocating the device and starting an audio recording on the victim's device. Clicking on the Ipec menu also displays a terminal we can use to send shell commands to the victim's system.

Once the BeEF framework hooks a browser, the possibilities are endless. We can do virtually anything. Therefore, it is important to be careful when clicking links and pop-up or flash messages.

METASPLOIT

The Metasploit framework is perhaps the larget, most complete penetration testing and security auditing tool today. This tool is an open source tool that is regularly updated with new modules for monitoring even the most recent vulnerabilities. Metasploit comes with the Kali Linux distro. It is written in Ruby, although when it was created it was written in Perl. This tool was developed by HD Moore in 2003 and was then sold to an IT company called Rapid7 in 2009.

Metasploit is an immensely powerful tool that has great versatility. To fully utilize Metasploit, you must be comfortable using the terminal, which is a console type window. However, there is an option that allows for the use of Metasploit in a GUI window. Armitage, an opensource tool, makes this possible, although it does not have the capacity to fully utilize all aspects of the Metasploit framework in an attack. The meterpreter in the Metasploit framework is a module that is dumped in the victim's system, making it easy for the hacker to control that PC and maintain access for future hacks in that system. Getting started with Metasploit on Kali Linux is as good as opening the terminal and typing "msfconsole" without the quotes.

Metasploit contains modules that can be used during a hack. Some of these modules are written by developers or contributors from the open source community. An important set of modules includes the payloads. The payloads are very important when it comes to performing attacks within the Metasploit framework. These payloads are codes that have been written so that the hacker can gain a foothold in the victim's computer. Perhaps the most popular among these payloads is the meterpreter. This particular payload is very powerful, as it leaves no trace of a hack on the system's drive. It exists solely on the victim's system memory.

Then there is the Exploits module. These exploits are codes that have been written and packed for specific flaws in a victim's operating system. Different exploits exist for different operating system flaws, so flaws that are targeted for one vulnerability would fail when used for another.

The encoders are modules that encode the different payloads deployed into the target system to avoid detection by the victim's antivirus, anti-spyware or other security tools.

Other modules available on the Metasploit framework are the Post modules (which allow the hacker to gather passwords, tokens and hashes), the Nops modules (most of which allow for 100 percent execution of the payload or exploit) and the Auxiliary modules (which do not fit into other categories).

This framework is quite robust, as many kinds of hacking procedures can be carried out. Several procedures are executed by combining the modules and making them work in different ways. A good way for a beginner to learn more about the Metasploit framework is to type "help" without the quotes in the Metasploit framework console.

Chapter 10 Strategies To Combat Cyber Terrorist Threats

Implement strategic plans to counter cyber terrorist efforts will ensure that your organization has the means to combat any threats it may face. There are a number of strategies which a business can employee or in order to stay ahead and heighten their security capabilities in the face of a threat. These are:

Prosecuting Perpetrators

Many attacks can behind the wall of anonymity with many smaller organizations failing to pursue and prosecute the hackers responsible. While this can be a costly activity, there are some advantages in identifying and taking the attackers to court. This can be a shock to the cyber terrorist community and set the standard for which other organizations should conduct themselves in the wake of an attack. If the case is particularly high profile, the organization can benefit from the hard-line response with the prosecuted hackers being an example to the rest of the criminal organizations that are determined to wreak havoc on your business. This example set can send waves throughout the rest of the community and can lead to improvements in the investigation and prosecution process of criminal cyber terrorists. Therefore, is always in the best

interest of the parties that have been affected by an attack to seek justice.

Develop New Security Practices

Take a Proactive Approach

It is important for both corporations and the general public to take a proactive approach as the threat from cyber terrorism becomes more sophisticated and targeted. This involves keeping up to date with the latest information within the cyber security sphere such as threats, vulnerabilities and noteworthy incidents as they will allow security professionals to gain a deeper insight into how these components could affect their organizations. From there they are able to develop and implement stronger security measures thereby reducing the opportunities for hackers to exploit for cyber-attacks.

Organizations should constantly be on the forefront of cyber security having a multi-level security infrastructure in order to protect valuable data and user's private information. All activities that are critical in nature should have security audits frequently to ensure all policies and procedures relating to security are adhered to. Security should be treated as an ongoing and continuous process rather than an aftermath of the consequences of an attack.

Deploy Vital Security Applications

There are many tools available for security professionals to protect their networks and they can provide a significant benefit to the job at hand. These applications involve firewalls, IDS, as well as anti-virus software that can ensure better protections against potential hackers. Using these security systems, security personnel are able to record, monitor and report any suspicious activities that can indicate the system is at risk. The applications are able to streamline the process, making the job far more efficient and effective. Utilizing these types of tools ensures that security personnel are assisted with the latest in prevention technology and have a greater probability of combating attackers.

Establish Business Disaster Recovery Plans

In the event that an attack does occur, all businesses should have a worst-case scenario contingency plan in place to ensure that processes and operations are brought back to normally as soon as possible. Without such plans, the consequences can be disastrous leading to a loss in revenue and reputation on behalf of the business. Once these plans have been devised, they should be rehearsed regularly in order to test their effectiveness and also provide staff with training in the event of an attack.

These plans should be comprised of two main components, these being, repair and restoration. From the perspective of repair, the attacking force should be neutralised as soon as possible with the objective to return operations to normalcy and have all functions up and running. The restoration element is geared towards having pre-specified arrangements with hardware, software as well as a network comprised of service vendors, emergency services and public utilities on hand to assist in the restoration process.

Cooperation with Other Firms

Your organization would not be alone in dealing with the aftermath of a cyber-attack. Many organizations exist in order to deal with cyber terrorism threats both public and private. These groups can go a long way in helping with issues relating to cyber terrorism such as improving the security within your organization, helping devise and implement disaster recovery plans and further discuss how you can deal with threats in the future and what this means for the wider community. Having this extended network available to you will enhance your efforts in resisting cyber-attacks as well as having a role in discussing other emerging threats and protecting organizations facing these same threats.

Increasing Security Awareness

It is important not to become complacent in times where security threats are prevalent and this requires an increase in awareness with all issues relating to cyber security. Having your organization become an authority in raising awareness within the community will help educate other organizations in how they can defend themselves against attacks and strengthen their own security which in turn will damage the cyberterrorist community as they face a stronger resistance. You can also raise awareness within your own organization through security training programs which will help all employees equip themselves with the right skillset to combat threats that could arise through their own negligence and will also help them be more alert in times when threats could be present.

Chapter 11 Tails

Edward Snowden. The name rings a bell for most people around the globe. In tech circles he is a visionary. As for the non-techies, a few labels come to mind: Whistleblower. Hero. Traitor. Regardless of what you pin him with, one thing is certain: He hates censorship and loves anonymity, the kind of anonymity that calls for untrackable execution. Before discussing anything, he insisted liaisons use not only *PGP* (pretty good privacy) but the end-all-be-all of anonymity tools: *Tails*-- a thief-simple tool that frustrates even those in the upper echelon of the NSA. And for good reason, since even they do not know the wizard who designed it.

Where Tor is the worm of the anonymous fisherman, Tails is the fishing box. The fish at the other end have no idea who is inside the boat, watching, listening. It's a hacker's tool but also a patriot weapon. Using it is a breeze: install it on a USB stick, CD, whatever, boot from said stick and find yourself cloaked and shielded from the NSA, provided that you don't out yourself. And if you're using Tails, you're smarter than that anyway.

Built upon the shell of Linux, it acts as an operating system and comes with an assortment of nukes to launch under Big Brother's nose: Tor browser, chat client, email, office suite and image/sound editor, among others.

Snowden preferred Tails on account of its no-write rule: no direct data writing. A breach from a remote adversary? Not going to happen. Forensics investigation? Nope. No trace is going to be left on the DVD/USB. Obviously this is a no brainer to use if you're an NSA employee looking to spill the beans on unconstitutional spying, as well as a must-have for political dissidents and journalists. It is armored with plausible deniability, the same as Truecrypt.

Tor runs like warm butter when you boot with Tails. There's not much of a learning curve, and no excessive tweaking required. You can use it in the same PC you use at work. Boot from USB or DVD. Do your thing then reboot back into your normal PC with no record or footprint of your Tailing. For all intents, you're a ghost on the internet. And speaking of ghosts, the creators of Tails are anonymous themselves. No one knows their identities. But what we do know is that they will not bow to governments trying to muscle a backdoor into the code.

Linus Torvalds, creator of Linux, said in 2013, "The NSA has been pressuring free software projects and developers in various ways," implying that they had made the effort, and all with taxpayer funds. A bit like the cat saying to the mouse, "Transparency is good for you. Sleep out in the open and not the damp and dark, flea-infested mousehole." They don't like secrets.

You might be asking, how do we *know* that Tails does not already *have* a backdoor? How do we know that the NSA has not already greased their hands? The evidence is twofold: the code is open-source (anyone can audit it), and the mere fact that the NSA made an effort to sideline end-users says they fear such a powerful package. They cannot peer inside to see what the mice are doing. Snowden claimed that the NSA, while he was with them, was a major thorn in the side of that organization.

At the time of Tails conception five years ago, the interest had already started to build up in the Tor community for a more cohesive toolbox. "At that time some of us were already Tor enthusiasts and had been involved in free software communities for years," they said. "But we felt that something was missing to the panorama: a toolbox that would bring all the essential privacy enhancing technologies together and made them ready to use and accessible to a larger public."

PGP is also included in package. You owe it to yourself and peace of mind to learn it. Spend a Sunday with it and you'll be a competent user. Spend a week and you'll be an enthusiast. As well, *KeePassX* can be useful if you want to store different info (usernames, pass phrases, sites, comments) into one database. These two are like a good set of gauntlets no aspiring black knight would do without. And don't think the blacksmiths have just smelted down some cheap metal, either. The designers have gone to a lot of trouble to modify the privacy and security settings. The more they do, the less you have to.

But the true Achilles heel is the *metadata*. Tails is really lousy at hiding it. It doesn't try to. It doesn't clear any of it nor does it encrypt the headers of your encrypted emails. Are you an ebook author? Be careful about PDFs and .mobi files, as depending on which software you use, it can store the author's name and creation date of your work. But this is not really the fault of Tails. Rather, it is the wishes of the development team to stay compatible with the SMTP protocol.

The other problem with metadata is pictures: JPEGs, TIFF, BITMAPS and so on, which again, depending on the software, can store EXIF data--data that stores the date the picture was taken as well as the GPS coordinates of the image. Newer cameras and mobile phones like Samsung Galaxy are notorious for this, and even keep a thumbnail of the EXIF data intact for nose parkers with nothing to do all day but to sniff through other people's property. A *fake GPS spoofer* may be useful but even that won't eliminate the exif data. You'll need a separate *app* for this. You might even go so far as to only use formats that don't store any metadata at all. Plain-text is one option, though even that can be watermarked.

You might think, "Can I hide Tails activity?" The short answer is: maybe. It depends on the resources of the adversary. And just who is the adversary? The government? The private detective? The employer? The fingerprint Tails leaves is far less visible than what Tor leaves. And yes, it is possible for an administrator to see you are using Tor, as well as your ISP. They cannot tell what you're doing on Tor, mind you, but there are Tor Browser Bundle users, and Tails users. It all comes down to the sites you visit.

We've seen how they can build a profile on you from your resolution, window metrics, addons and extensions and time zones and fonts, but to alleviate this the Tails developers have tried to make everyone look the same, as if they were all wearing white Stormtrooper armor. Some fall through the cracks, making themselves easier for a correlation attack by installing too many addons and thus marking themselves in the herd: A purple-colored stormtrooper, if you will. Such and such user has a nice font enhancer while no other user does. This alone does not break anonymity, but with a hundred other factors and sufficient resources, it might be the one detail that breaks the house of cards. Death by a thousand stings.

You might find Tor *bridges* (alternative entry points on Tor) to be a good investment in reading, as they can better hide you from your ISP. In fact, using a bridge makes it considerably harder for your ISP to even know you are using Tor. If you decide this route (and you should if merely using Tor can get you arrested-- a case in which you should NOT use the default Tor configuration), the bridge address must be known.

Be mindful of the fact that a few bridges can be obtained on the Tor website. If you know about it, others do too--even adversaries like the NSA, but it is still stronger for anonymity purposes than the default Tor config. Like Freenet, it would be optimal if you personally know someone in a country outside the USA who runs a private obfuscated bridge that has the option *PublishServerDescriptor 0*. As always, luck favors the prepared.

Chapter 12 The Final Report

It is time now to send the client a final report with your feedback on all accomplished tasks.

It is important to stress how fundamental this part is. We need to present in a clear and complete manner all the information we gathered as well as each suggestion that could help to correct the weaknesses we spotted.

In addition to the list of vulnerabilities found and exploits used, we should include a part related to the so-called "remediation".

This part is meant to show the customer all the possible remedies for the risks we discovered.

It would be better to start the report with a general overview of the actions taken and then gradually enter into detail.

In this way, the report becomes easier to read for members of the management board and non-technicians, who will be able to understand exactly what is been reported.

Although we can also include other parts, a well-structured report usually consists of the following sections:

- Executive summary.
- Methodology used.

- Detailed analysis of the results.

Executive Summary

The executive summary is the report that can be understood even by non-technical staff, for example by managers.

First of all, we should define the scope and the estimated duration of this task.

By defining the scope of this task, we want to know exactly what type of penetration test we should perform and even more importantly what are the IP addresses or websites that we should include.

We must point out the evidences found and their level of criticality. We also need to prepare a graph showing the risk distribution according to the different variables:

Methodology

The methodology used integrates all the phases from the definition of the test scope to the final report.

We can summarize the procedure as follows:

- Definition of the test scope.
- Information gathering.
- Network scanning.
- Vulnerability assessment.
- Exploitation.
- Post exploitation.

- Other optional tests.
- Drafting of the report also through the use of automatic tools, for example with Dradis. (https://dradisframework.com/ce/).

As a side note, the report must also contain all the results you achieved that were related to the Web, including the **SQL Injection and XSS Cross Site Scripting**, which were not explained in this book.

You might also want to include the social engineering techniques you eventually used.

Detailed Analysis of The Results

The first task to complete in this sub-phase is defining the risk level of the various vulnerabilities you detected:

Then you can enlist all the vulnerabilities:

You can then conclude your report by mentioning the solutions and the suggestions that could help to block these risks and eradicate these problems.

Chapter 13 Banner Grabbing

This information will be useful to us in the next phase where we will look for vulnerabilities. In particular, the outdated version of a service could be exploited by a potential hacker.

We will start from the services normally associated with standard ports, and then move on the ones linked to unconventional ports.

Also, in this case we rely on a wizard that will lead us to define a specific service, make it active and try to grab the banner.

Installing The Web Server Microsoft Iis

We proceed with the installation of the IIS Web server directly from a **Windows Server 2012**.

You can refer to the following link for the installation steps: https://docs.microsoft.com/en-us/iis/get-started/whats-   new-in-iis-8/8-installing-iis-on-windows-server-2012

At the end of the installation process, you can open your browser and type: *"http://127.0.0.1"*. If everything went well, this is what should appear on your screen:

We can see that IIS is listening by executing the "netstat" command and listening on port 80.

With the and filtering by port 80, we can see how the latter is listening:

Banner Visualization In Microsoft Iis

At this point, we must be able to grab the banner of our web server so that we can detect its type and version.

First of all, let's connect to the Web server using "*telnet*":

Once the channel has been set up, we can enter two commands that allow us to interact with the web server:

- GET / HTTP/1.1
- HOST: 127.0.0.1

This is what will appear on your screen:

We have captured the banner of our IIS web server. We can now identify the type of service and its version. This information will be useful during the vulnerability assessment phase.

Banner Configuration On Kfsensor

We should now use KFSensor to simulate a Microsoft IIS type web server.

Once the configuration is complete, we can use the Nmap feature called "**service detection**", which will attempt to grab the banner of the listening service and inform us of what version it is.

Nmap has correctly grabbed the banner and detected the exact version of the simulated service.

Installing A Ftp Server

We have previously installed a Microsoft web server. Now, instead, we will have to install an FTP server. You can find the installation steps at the following link:
https://social.technet.microsoft.com/wiki/contents/articles/12364.windows-server-2012-ftp-installation.aspx

Once the installation is complete, we can proceed with the creation of a new **FTP** site:

We are now listening port 21 without using SSL:

Ftp Banner Grabbing With Nmap

We can now capture the *FTP banner* using the Nmap service detection feature:

As you can see from the screenshot above, we have correctly detected the version of the FTP service running on the target machine.

Note that some system administrators may decide to obfuscate the banner for a certain service. We can also do this on the FTP server defined above:

Now we will no longer be able to detect the version of the service with Nmap:

Nmap was able to understand that port 21 is open. However, it does not provide any information about the version of the service running.

Ftp Banner Grabbing Wirh Metasploit

It is a tool that is used in the exploitation phase of a system. However, there are a number of additional modules that allow you to perform other activities, such as banner grabbing.

We start Metasploit by launching the "*msf*" command from terminal. Then we type the following command:

In "*rhost*", we need to enter the IP address of the victim machine, that is where the listening FTP service is located.

Once this part is completed, we can run the "**exploit**" command and then start the scanner:

The scan is quickly completed, and the result obtained informs us of the presence of a *Microsoft FTP server*. We grabbed the banner once again.

Ftp Banner Grabbing With Netcat

NETCAT is another useful tool used for grabbing banners. You can click here to learn more: https://en.wikipedia.org/wiki/Netcat.

Below is the command used to grab the banner:

Ftp Banner Grabbing With Telnet

We have already seen how the Telnet command works. Let's use it now to grab a banner:

Even in this case, we are able to correctly detect and grab the banner.

Operating System Detection

In addition to detecting a certain running service, it is also important to know the operating system present on a given machine.

We can follow two different procedures:

- Active mode.
- Passive mode.

In the active mode, we interact directly with the target. Nmap is a tool commonly used in active mode.

On the other hand, the passive mode listens to network traffic. Based on the characteristics of each operating system, we can obtain fairly precise information. A tool that works in this mode is "**P0f**" (https://it.wikipedia.org/wiki/P0f).

Os Detection With Nmap

Let's see how to detect the operating system of a certain machine using Nmap. The option to use is "-o", so this command will be the command we need to execute:

By running this command, we will examine only the first 100 doors and try to detect the operating system.

The result is the following:

Nmap was able to identify that the operating system in use is probably Windows and specifically version 7, 2012 or 8.1.

For more details, you might have to use other tools as well.

Os Detection With Xprobe

XPROBE is another tool useful for detecting the operating system. This is the command we should execute:

We should see the following results:

We are dealing with a Linux operating system, probably with 2.6.11 kernel.

Os Detection With P0f

As anticipated, this tool allows to perform a passive operating system detection. In this case, we do not need to interact directly with the target machine.

We need to capture some network traffic, so that **P0f** can complete the detection process. This is the command we should execute:

We press "*send*" and place the tool on hold:

We generate random traffic using, for example, the netcat:

This is the screen we will see if the traffic generated is enough for P0f:

As you can see, P0f informs us of what operating system version is currently used on the machine.

.

Chapter 14 Enumeration

Enumeration is an important phase of the penetration test process. It consists in exploiting the characteristics of a certain service in order to obtain as much information as possible.

There are services that work well with this type of investigation, such as

- SMTP, TCP port 25.
- DNS, UDP port 53.
- SNMP, UDP port 161.
- NETBIOS, UDP port 137,138; TCP port 139.

In this chapter, we will examine enumeration related to the following services:

- NETBIOS enumeration.
- DNS enumeration.
- Enumeration through DEFAULT PASSWORD.

Enumeration With Netbios

Netbios is a protocol that operates at the session layer of the **ISO/OSI model**. This protocol allows us to explore the network resources of computers, printers or files.

We can use Netbios to extract several information, including the following:

- *Hostname.*
- *Username.*

- *Domain.*
- *Printers.*
- Available network folders.

First of all, we should use Nmap to confirm that the TCP ports 139 and 445 are actually open:

nmap -v -p 139,445 192.169.1.120

After completing this step, we can use a special command, the **NBTSCAN**, to investigate systems with **open ports 139,445.**

We have a whole range of extracted **NETBIOS** information.

We can refer to another Windows command - "net view" - to continue our investigation on a specific host:

net view 192.168.1.10

It gives us the list of shared resources on our target. The *"net use"* command allows us to access these resources.

Nmap contains many scripts that can be used to enumerate NETBIOS. You can find them on the following path: /usr/share/nmap/scripts.

These are the scripts we need to verify any NETBIOS vulnerabilities:

- *smb-vuln-conficker.*
- *smb-vuln-cve2009-3103.*
- *smb-vuln-ms06-025.*

- *smb-vuln-ms07-029.*
- *smb-vuln-regsvc-dos.*
- *smb-vuln-ms08-067.*

Enumeration With Dns

With a single command we can extract different DNS records, which are the following ones:

- *SOA.*
- *A.*
- *MX.*
- *NS.*
- *CNAME.*
- *PTR.*
- *HINFO.*
- *TXT.*

We need to run this command:

dnsenum domain.com

Enumeration With Default Password

Network devices – such as routers and switches – very often have a default password. These passwords are defined directly by the device manufacturer. I would obviously suggest you change them as soon as possible.

DefaultPassword is one of the many sites where default device passwords are stored (https://default-password.info/).

This website is very easy to use. You just need to select the device model and manufacturer:

Chapter 15 Vulnerability Assessment

Thanks to network scanning, banner grabbing, and enumeration, we should have at this point a pretty good understanding of the types of services running on our network.

Now it's time to look for any vulnerabilities and we will use specific tools to carry out this activity.

A part of this research should be carried out manually, while we can use some tools to automate other parts of this process.

At this link, you can find a detailed report written by **SANS** that lists all the steps we should take to perform a *vulnerability Assessment:* https://www.sans.org/reading-room/whitepapers/basics/vulnerability-assessment-421.

I also want to clarify that, unlike vulnerability assessment, a penetration test has the additional purpose of exploiting the vulnerabilities found.

Below is the list of tools we will use:

- *Nessus.* https://www.tenable.com/products/nessus-vulnerability-scanner.

- *Nexpose.* https://www.rapid7.com/products/nexpose/.
- *OpenVAS.* http://www.openvas.org/.

Installing Nessus

There are two available versions of **Nessus**: a paid one and a free one. We will obviously refer to the second one.

We start by going to https://www.tenable.com/products/nessus-vulnerability-scanner and downloading this software.

At this stage we need to obtain an activation code that validates the license we are using. Just click on "Get an Activation Code" as you can see from the screenshot here below:

You will receive an e-mail with the activation code within a short period of time. Once the installation is complete, a browser window will open and point to: **http://127.0.0.1:8834.**

You will then need to enter the activation code that was provided to you:

If all went well, we should now be able to start using this software.

Scanning With Nessus

Nessus has a set of pre-compiled scans that you just need to execute:

We can use KFSensor to test the vulnerabilities of our victim machine.

Once scanned, this is the first detected vulnerability:

More in detail:

To confirm this, we can verify that the service is simulated on KFSensor:

Below is an overview of the vulnerabilities found:

An interesting feature is the possibility to create an exportable report in .pdf format:

Installing Nexpose

At this step, we need to download the Nexpose software and type the free license key.

We can run this software by connecting to the following link: **https: // localhost: 3780.**

Once we open this software, we can perform various actions:

Scanning With Nexpose

The first action we need to take is to create a site:

We can specify the type of scan to be performed:

The scan results can be summarized as follows:

In the image below we can see a detailed list of the vulnerabilities found:

Nexpose offers us the possibility to create easy interactions with, for example, Metasploit.

We can also see enough details about each vulnerability:

We are also provided with suggestions regarding the remediation phase, which is meant to find a remedy to the vulnerabilities found:

Here too, we have the possibility to generate a customizable report:

Websites For Vulnerability Search

Here is a list of websites you can refer to for more details about each vulnerability:

- *Exploit Database.* https://www.exploit-db.com/.
- *Security Focus.* http://www.securityfocus.com/.
- *Packet Storm.* https://packetstormsecurity.com/.
- *CVE Details.* http://www.cvedetails.com/.

Chapter 16 Learning How to Carry Out an Effective Attack

Now that you have a good understanding of hacking concepts and what is involved in the penetration of a system as well as how you can turn hacking into a career, we want to get into the heart of the action and learning how to carry out an effective attack. This is for demonstration purposes to help strengthen your knowledge and ideally stem further education. If you are still unsure on the basics of hacking, have a read through and study this book thoroughly as we will be going through this step by step guide with the assumption that you have a solid grasp of the topics of hacking and computer security and we wouldn't want you to get lost along the way.

Before you do get started, you will need to utilize a tool to help with the pen-test. For this example, we will be using Metasploit, an open source tool which has a number of functions which pen-testers and black hat hackers alike will find incredibly useful. The tool has a database filled with a large number of known exploits which can be picked up during the vulnerability test by the variety of scanners. Metasploit is one of the more popular pen-testing software applications and as an open source program, there is a large community which you can interact with in case you have any questions or concerns.

For the purpose of this example, we will be hacking into a virtual machine as this is a great way to practice and scan for weaknesses without actually breaking into an established machine. We will be scanning our virtual machine for exploits upon which we will then penetrate the system and extract the information we require. The virtual machine will also have limited access meaning it won't actually be accessible as easy to other people who may be scanning your network, leaving you in complete control. In order to create a virtual machine, we will be using VirtualBox, a software that allows you to establish a hacking lab in order to test your skills on a simulated machine. VirtualBox is another open source software that allows you to have access to the source code free of charge, allowing you to customise your build to your specifications.

Before continuing with your experiment ensure that the techniques and tools you use throughout this test are confined only to your machine and never used on other computers as this is not only illegal, it is also potentially dangerous. Even if you are simply learning how to carry out an attack for the purpose of your own education, if you are caught you can be prosecuted, and as you should have a good understanding from reading this book, this can be quite a serious crime and yes, it is possible to be caught. Keeping this in mind, let us go through with our virtual pen-test.

Initial Preparation

The first step toward setting up your environment is creating virtual machine to run on VirtualBox. You will need two machines, a target and a victim. You are able to download these online, they will come with files that we can extract as well as vulnerabilities to exploit. Once you have the files in place, extract them and create a new machine on VirtualBox and choose the type of machine you will be using. From there you decide how much RAM your machine will be running with, this isn't too important so selecting a small amount won't affect your test, 512MB is a good starting point.

Your next task is then to select a hard disk by checking the Use an Existing Disk option. You are able to click on the folder option and select the appropriate file that you had extracted from your download files and once that is all done, click create and your virtual machine and you are ready to move onto the next step.

Creating a Network

In order to access your machine, you will need to establish a virtual network. This is to keep your machine safe from existing threats outside your control. You are able to do this through VirtualBox by going through File > Preferences > Network >

Host Only Network. Once you click the plus sign, you are able to add a new entry which will be your virtual network. Now is time to add your virtual machine to the virtual network. You are able to do this by selecting your virtual machine and clicking settings from the menu. From there you will see the network tab which will allow you to click 'Attacked to' from and Host-Only Adaptor from the drop-down menu.

Attacking Tools

Now that your network and machine have been set up it is time to acquire the tools to launch your attack. In this example, we will be using Kali as it is simple to set up and you can also run it live in a virtual machine. Once you have downloaded Kali as an ISO file, open VirtualBox and click Add to allow you to create another machine which will be your attacker. For your attacker, you want to allocate some more memory to the machine of around 2GB, if your machine has less than 4GB on the system, you may need to allocate less. You will not need to allocate any hard drive space, Kali is running live so check the box Do Not Add a Virtual Hard Drive. Once you are ready, hit create and your offending machine will be created. Ensure that you attach the machine to your network and change the adapter to host-holy. From here, you will start both machines and run Kali on your attack machine when prompted to add a bootable CD. You are then presented with the interface, and are ready to start scanning and gathering information from the Kali desktop interface.

Gathering Information

The next step in carrying out your attack is deciding upon your target. For the purpose of this experiment, we will be carrying out the attack on our victim server. In reality, this is a simple surface attack rather than focusing on the entire network that we had set up or the virtualization tools. From there it is time to gather information to discover the vulnerabilities that we will be exploiting. In order to do this, we will need to set this up in the software. This is where Metasploit will come into play as our framework for carrying out the pen-test, taking us through the process.

It is now time to begin collecting information. To do this, we must first we must initiate the services through Kali by entering:

"service postgresql start"

"service metasploit start"

Metasploit is best used through the console interface known as MSFConsole which is opened with

"Msfconsole"

Now you are ready to start your scan.

Scanning for Ports

In order to gather information on ports, you can use Nmap which is built into MSFconsole. In order to set this up, you will first need to enter the IP address of the target which you can find by typing in

"ifconfig"

This will then bring up information on the IP address, labelled inet addr within the eth0 block. The IP address should be similar to other machines found on your network. By running a scan of the IP address by using

Db_map -sS -A *TARGET IP ADDRESS*

You are able to have detailed list of all services running on the machine. From there you are able gather further information on each of the services to discover any vulnerabilities to exploit. Once you have found the weakest point, you are able to move into attack mode.

Exploitation

By enter services into MSFconsole, you are able to access the database of information on the services running on the machine. Once you have discovered a service that is particularly vulnerable, you are able to scan this service to assess points of weakness. This is done by typing

Search *service name*

Once you have done this, you will be provided a list of exploits which you can take advantage and can then tell MSFconsole to exploit the model. Once you have set the target, you simply need to type the command "run" for the program to work its magic and access the port. You will then be able to see what you are able to do once operating from the computer with a number of commands at your disposal with the permissions provided to you by the service. From here you are able to extract data as well as upload data depending on your objective.

Once you have accessed the machine, you will obviously want to ensure that you remained in control and fortunately Metasploit has a number of tools to assist.

Having a deeper understanding of the meaning behind the word hacker can open up new doors for you not just within your career if you decide to explore IT security but also within your business and personal life as you become better equipped in dealing with external threats to your networks and systems. Before reading this book, you like many other people, may have had some misconceptions about what hacking actually means, who is behind it, why they do it, what they have to gain from it and what can be done to prevent them.

Now that you have reached the end of our book on hacking, you should have a much greater insight into the world of hacking including what it means to be an ethical hacker and how they operate. Knowing that an ethical hacker is also known as a white hat hacker, you also learnt the difference between white and black hat hackers, who are motivated by personal reasons whether that could be financial or ideological. You also gained some insight into the hackers that lie on the boundaries of ethics such as those known as grey hats and red hats as well the hacktivists that so often capture our awareness in the media.

We also explored the techniques used by hackers to attack your computer and what each of these attacks can do to a system, the seriousness behind them and the types of hackers that employ these tactics to achieve their motivations. Upon learning these techniques, you also learnt how it was possible to avoid becoming a target through precautions which can protect your system and the information contained on it.

We then moved onto the topic on penetration testing and how organizations are able to simulate attacks on their own systems in order to expose weaknesses and vulnerabilities that could be exploited by external hackers. We learnt the basic process of how a pen-test works and why it is performed. This gave us some insight into the world of ethical hackers and what their job is comprised of. Once learning this, we took a deeper look into careers in IT security, how the indri is moving and the qualifications that are widely recognised in the industry.

We then took a look at the other side of the coin into the world of cyber terrorism. We explored the reasoning's behind why terrorists carry out these attacks as well as how organizations are able to better equip themselves for dealing with these threats. In looking at each type of attack, we gained an understand how businesses need to be extra vigilant to avoid suffering losses both financial and intangible.

Towards the end of the book we walked through the basic setup of a pen-test and how it can be performed using a lab type scenario on a virtual machine. While this was just a brief cover of a pen-test, it hopefully spurred some curiosity for you to continue your education further and develop new skills in hacking. With the now solid understanding of hacking in your possession, it is worth exploring further certifications and courses that will allow you to get closer to a career in security as a white hat hacker and expressing your skills in a healthy environment or just to expand your knowledge and become more aware.

Conclusion

I want to thank you once again for choosing this book.

Kali Linux is a very advanced flavor of Linux, which is used for Security Auditing and Penetration Testing. After all the tools that we have looked at, it is pretty clear that if you want to succeed in the domain of Security Research, Kali Linux will provide with unlimited power to achieve the same. It is also clear that if you are just beginning with Linux, Kali Linux is not the place that you would want to start with as it is a highly complex operating system created and aimed at achieving one goal and that is security.

PYTHON FOR BEGINNERS:

Introduction

Basics of Programming

Before we take a plunge into the world of computer programming, let us take a closer look at what computer programs are and what they are supposed to be. The standard defining of a computer program is as follows:

> A sequence of instructions for performing a particular task that has been written in a specific programming language is commonly referred to as a computer program.

As you can see in the given definition, two phrases have been written in bold namely, 'sequence of instructions' and 'programming language'. To understand the meaning and significance of these two terms, let us take an example. For instance, you have a household help and you have to tell her the procedure to prepare 2 cups of coffee. What will be the set of instructions that you will give to her? In all probability, you will tell her something like this –

1. Firstly, take two cups and keep them on the kitchen slab.

2. Take a boiling pan and using one of these cups for measurement, add two cups of water to it.

3. Switch on the stove.

4. Put the boiling pan on medium heat and wait until the water starts boiling.

5. In the two cups, add 1 teaspoon of coffee, 1 teaspoon of sugar and 1 teaspoon of milk powder.

6. Add boiling water to the cups.

7. Lastly, serve.

The seven steps mentioned above form what can be called 'human program'. It is a set of instructions that you have given to a human to perform a specific task. Since the language used for this human program is English, the programming language used for writing this human program is English. If your household help doesn't understand English, this human program will fail. Therefore, you will have to translate this program to the language she understands, which can be French, Arabic, Hindi, Spanish or any other language for that matter.

Analogously, when you have to tell the computer to do something for you, you have to give it a set of instructions in the language that it can understand. The language that it understands is the computer programming language and the set of instructions written in that language and given to the computer to perform a specific task is simply a computer program.

There are some other terms that you may also encounter in the world of computer programming. One such term is software. A computer program is usually also referred to as software. Besides this, you may also see phrases like source code and program coding. These are terms usually used for referring to the set of instructions written in a computer program.

Computer Programs

Computer programs are the heart and soul of a computer. The hardware is just a dead body unless you have active computer programs running on the system. All the capabilities of the computer can be used only after you tell the computer what it should do for you in the form of computer programs.

We unconsciously use many computer programs everyday. For instance, Google Chrome or Internet Explorer that you use to browse Internet is a computer program. The chat programs you use on your computer or mobile phone is a computer program. Moreover, the voice calls and SMS capabilities of mobile phones are also computer programs. You name it and there is a computer program associated with it. Whenever and whenever you use a computer to do a task, you are using a computer program.

Since computer programming is a skilled job, the individual who has an expertise in computer programming is referred to as a computer programmer. Depending on the programming language in which the computer programmer has expertise, he or she is called Python/C/HTML/Java/CSS/SQL/JavaScript programmer.

Algorithm

Now that you are thorough with the concept of computer program, you can simply relate computer programming to the process and art of writing computer programs. These programs should not only perform the specified task, but they should also do them well. This is where the concept of effective and efficient programming came into existence.

In order to make the process of program designing simpler, several approaches have been designed. The systematic procedure developed to solve a problem is called an algorithm. It is one of the most effective approaches for creation of a sequence of well-defined instructions aimed towards performing a task. You will hear this term just as much as you shall counter computer programs as they essentially go hand in hand.

In simple words, an algorithm is an English language equivalent of the computer program, written in the form of a list, by the programmer, before transforming it into a programming language – specific code. A sample algorithm has been given below to help you understand how an algorithm typically looks like. This algorithm given below computes the largest number from a list of numbers.

Algorithm for Computing Largest Number From Given List of Numbers

1. Get the given list of numbers.
2. Assume a variable L, which will hold the largest number.
3. Initialize L with the first number of the list.
4. Go to the next number of the list.
5. If L is less than this number, put this new number in L
6. Repeat step 4 and step 5 till the list is completely scanned.
7. Print L on the screen

This is a raw algorithm written in simple language to make it easy to understand for beginners. There is a standard procedure that needs to be followed for writing algorithms. However, this is part of advanced programming fundamentals and is beyond the scope of this book.

Programming Languages

Just like we have innumerable languages that are used for communication between humans, scientists have developed a plethora of computer programming languages to serve and meet the varied requirements of developers and applications.

We will introduce some of the key languages to you in the chapters to come. A list of the programming languages that we shall cover is as follows –

1. Java
2. SQL
3. C
4. C++
5. C#
6. Python
7. HTML
8. CSS
9. JavaScript

In order to understand the concept of programming languages, their structure and how they work, let us look at English, which is a standard human interface language. It is used by billions of people around the world to communicate with each other. As we know, English language makes words from a set of alphabets and these words are used to make sentences.

In order to make sure that the sentences are understandable to one and all, several grammar rules have to be applied. Besides this, language elements like conjunctions, verbs, nouns and adverbs, in addition to several others, have to be kept in mind while forming sentences. Likewise, other languages like French, Spanish, Russian, Arabic or Hindi also have their own set of rules that need to be followed for effective communication between two humans.

In the same manner, computer languages also have rules and elements that need to be understood before you can write programs to communicate with the computer. Some of these basic elements are as follows –

- Syntax
- Data types
- Keywords
- Variables
- Operators
- Loops
- Decision Making
- Program organization elements like Functions
- File I/O
- Programming environment

Most of the languages that we shall deal with in this book will have most of these elements. However, how they are included in the programming language varies. In this book, we shall introduce you to the different programming languages listed above and deal with the different elements and advanced programming concepts specific to the programming language in books specifically written for the language.

Chapter 1 Programming Environment

Although, programming environment does not form one of the core elements of a programming language, it would not be wrong to state that it is one of the prerequisites that you need to learn and get acquainted with even before you have written your first program. You will never know if your program is right or wrong unless you have a programming environment that can test the same for you. This is the reason why we are going to introduce you to programming environment before we jump to languages.

Simply, programming environment is software that will allow you to create, compile and execute computer programs on the system. It is an interface between the programmer and the computer, which will convert the programs that you will write into the computer's language and ask it to execute the same for you. Therefore, before you pick up any programming language, be sure to enquire about the required programming environment and how the same can be set up on the computer that you intend to use for your programming course.

Digging deeper into the programming environment and its setup, it is made up of three basic elements namely text editor, compiler and interpreter. In all probability, you will need all these three components for your course. So, before you go searching for them, let us help you understand what they exactly are and why you will need them.

Text Editor

A text editor is a simple text program that will allow you to create text files in which you will write you code. Depending on the programming language you are working on, the extension of the text file will change. For instance, if you programming in C language, your text files will have the extension .c.

If you are working on a Windows machine, you can simply search for Notepad in the search bar and use it as a text editor for your programs. You can also explore Notepad++ for some advanced options. It is freely available and you will just need to download and install it on your machine. On the other hand, if you are a Mac user, you can explore text editor options like BBEdit and TextEdit.

Compiler

Now that you have written the program and you are all ready to test if you have written it correctly or not, you have to give it to the computer and see if it understands what you are trying to communicate. However, the computer only understands binary language and what you have written is far from what it can directly digest. Therefore, this file needs to be converted into binary format.

If you have made syntactical errors and not followed the rules of the programming language, the compiler will not be able to make this conversion smoothly and will raise an error message for you. Therefore, the compiler is a program that checks if you have followed the syntactical rules of the chosen programming language and converts the text file into its binary form. Moreover, this process of conversion is referred to as compilation.

Most programming languages like C, Java, C++ and Pascal, besides many others require compilation and you will need to install their respective compilers before you can execute any programs written using them.

Interpreter

Unlike the programming languages mentioned above, there are some other programming languages like Python and Perl that do not require compiler. Therefore, instead of a compiler, they need an interpreter, which is also software. The interpreter simply reads the program from the text file and as it parses the file, it converts the contents of the file and executes them. If you are working on any such programming languages, remember to install the corresponding interpreter on your system before starting.

If you haven't worked with a computer before or have little to no experience in installing software on the computer, technical advice from an expert is recommended. However, be sure to do the installation yourself, as it will help you build an acquaintance with the device that you will work with in the near future.

Besides this, if your computer does not support installation of any of the programming environment elements, you can also make use of the online compilers and interpreters that are available for all the different programming languages nowadays. All you need is a good Internet connection and a web browser to open these online facilities and get started with your programming lessons and practice sessions right away.

Chapter 2 Data Analysis with Python

Another topic that we need to explore a bit here is how Python, and some of the libraries that come with it, can work with the process of data analysis. This is an important process for any businesses because it allows them to take all of the data and information they have been collecting for a long time, and then can put it to good use once they understand what has been said within the information. It can be hard for a person to go through all of this information and figure out what is there, but for a data analyst who is able to use Python to complete the process, it is easy to find the information and the trends that you need.

The first thing that we need to look at here though is what data analysis is all about. Data analysis is going to be the process that companies can use in order to extract out useful, relevant, and even meaningful information from the data they collect, in a manner that is systematic. This ensures that they are able to get the full information out of everything and see some great results in the process. There are a number of reasons that a company would choose to work on their own data analysis, and this can include:

- Parameter estimation, which helps them to infer some of the unknowns that they are dealing with.
- Model development and prediction. This is going to be a lot of forecasting in the mix.
- Feature extraction which means that we are going to identify some of the patterns that are there.
- Hypothesis testing. This is going to allow us to verify the information and trends that we have found.
- Fault detection. This is going to be the monitoring of the process that you are working on to make sure that there aren't any biases that happen in the information.

One thing that we need to make sure that we are watching out for is the idea of bias in the information that we have. If you go into the data analysis with the idea that something should turn out a certain way, or that you are going to manipulate the data so it fits the ideas that you have, there are going to be some problems. You can always change the data to say what you would like, but this doesn't mean that you are getting the true trends that come with this information, and you may be missing out on some of the things that you actually need to know about.

This is why a lot of data analysts will start this without any kind of hypothesis at all. This allows them to see the actual trends that come with this, and then see where the information is going to take you, without any kind of slant with the information that you have. This can make life easier and ensures that you are actually able to see what is truly in the information, rather than what you would like to see in that information.

Now, there are going to be a few different types of data that you can work with. First, there is going to be the deterministic. This is going to also be known as the data analysis that is non-random. And then there is going to be the stochastic, which is pretty much any kind that is not going to fit into the category of deterministic.

The Data Life Cycle

As we go through this information, it is important to understand some of the different phases that come with the data life cycle. Each of these comes together to ensure that we are able to understand the information that is presented to us and that we are able to use all of the data in the most efficient and best way possible.

There are a few stages that are going to come with this data life cycle, and we are going to start out with some of the basics to discuss each one to help us see what we are able to do with the data available to us. First, we work with data capture. The first experience that an individual or a company should have with a data item is to have it pass through the firewalls of the enterprise. This is going to be known as the Data Capture, which is basically going to be the act of creating values of data that do not exist yet and have never actually existed in that enterprise either. There are three ways that you can capture the data including:

- Data acquisition: This is going to be the ingestion of data that is already existing that was produced by the organization but outside of the chosen enterprise.
- Data entry: This is when we are dealing with the creation of new data values to help with the enterprise and it is done by devices or human operators that can help to generate the data needed.
- Signal reception: This is where we are going to capture the data that a device has created with us, typically in the control system, but can be found in the Internet of Things if we would like.

The next part is going to be known as Data Maintenance. This is going to be where you supply the data to points at which data synthesis and data usage can occur in the next few steps. And it is best if you are able to work out the points so that they are going to be ready to go in this kind of phase.

What we will see during the data maintenance is that we are working to process the data, without really working to derive any value out of it yet. This is going to include integration changed data, cleansing, and making sure that the data is in the right format and as complete as possible before we get started. This ensures that no matter what method or algorithm you choose to work with here, you are going to be able to have the data ready to go.

Once you have been able to maintain the data and get it all cleaned up, it is time to work on the part known as data synthesis. This is a newer phase in the cycle and there are some places where you may not see this happen. This is going to be where we create some of the values of data through inductive logic, and using some of the data that we have from somewhere else as the input. The data synthesis is going to be the arena of analytics that is going to use modeling of some kind to help you get the right results in the end.

Data usage comes next. This data usage is going to be the part of the process where we are going to apply the data as information to tasks that the enterprise needs to run and then handle the management on its own. This would be a task that normally falls outside of your life cycle for the data. However, data is becoming such a central part of the model for most businesses and having this part done can make a big difference.

For example, the data itself can be a service or a product, or at least part of this service or product. This would then make it a part of the data usage as well. The usage of the data is going to have some special challenges when it comes to data governance. One of these is whether it is legal to use the data in the ways that most people in business would like. There could be some issues like contractual or regulatory constraints on how we can use this data and it is important that these are maintained as much as possible.

Once we have figured out the data usage, it is time to move on to data publication. In being used, it may be possible that our single data value may be sent outside of the enterprise. This is going to be known as the data publication, which we can define as the sending of data to a location that is not within the enterprise.

A good example of this would be when you have a brokerage that sends out some monthly statements to their client. Once the data has been sent outside the enterprise, it is de facto impossible to get that information back. When the values of data are wrong and you publish it, it is impossible to correct them because they are now beyond the reach of your enterprise. The idea of Data Governance, like we talked about before, is going to have to handle how this information that is incorrect can be handled with.

Next on the list is the data archival. We will see that the single data value that we are working with can sometimes experience a lot of different rounds of usage and then publication, but eventually, it is going to reach the very end of its life. The first part of this means that we need to be able to take the value of the data and archive it. When we work on the process of Data Archival, it is going to mean that we are copying the data to an environment where it is stored in case we need it again, in an active production environment, and then we will remove the data from all of those active environments as well.

This kind of archive for the data is simply going to be a place where the data is stored, but where no publication, usage, or maintenance is going to happen. If necessary, it is possible to take any of the data that is in the archive and bring it back out to use again.

And finally, we reach the part of data purging. This is going to be the end that comes with our single data value and the life cycle that it has gone through. Data purging is going to be when we remove every copy of data from the enterprise. If possible, you will reach this information through the archive. If there is a challenge from Data Governance at this point, it is just there to prove that the information and the data have gone through the proper purging procedure at that time.

–

Working with data analysis and why it is important

With this in mind, we need to pay attention to why we would want to work on data analysis to start with? Do we really need to be able to look through all of this information to find the trends, or is there another method? Let's look at an example of what can happen when we do this data analysis and why you would want to use it.

Let's consider that we are looking at a set of data that includes information about the weather that occurred across the globe between the years 2015 to 2018. We are also going to have information that is base don the country between these years as well. So, there is going to be a percentage of ran within that country and we are going to have some data that concerns this in our set of data as well.

Now, what if you would like to go through all of that data, but you would like to only take a look at the data that comes with one specific country. Let's say that you would like to look at America and you want to see what percentage of rain it received between 2016 and 2017. Now, how are you going to get this information in a quick and efficient manner?

What we would need to do to make sure that we were able to get ahold of this particular set of data is to work with the data analysis. There are several algorithms, especially those that come from machine learning, that would help you to figure out the percentage of rain that America gets between 2016 to 2017. And this whole process is going to be known as what data analysis is really all about.

The Python Panda Library

When it comes to doing some data analysis in Python, the best extension that you can use is Pandas. This is an open-sourced library that works well with Python and it is going to provide you with a high level of performance, data structures that are easy for even a beginner to use, and tools to make data analysis easy with Python. There are a lot of things to enjoy about this language, and if you want to be able to sort through all of the great information that you have available with the help of Python, then this is the library that you need to work with.

There are a lot of things that you can enjoy when it comes to working on the Python library. First off, this is one of the most popular and easy to use libraries when it comes to data science and it is going to work on top of the NumPy library. The name of Pandas that was given to this library is derived from the word of Panel Data, which is going to be an Econometrics from Multidimensional data. And one thing that a lot of coders are going to like about working with Pandas is that it is able to take a lot of the data that you need, including a SQL database or a TSV and CSV file, and will use it to create an object in Python. This object is going to have columns as well as rows called the data frame, something that looks very similar to what we see with a table in statistical software including Excel.

There are many different features that are going to set Pandas apart from some of the other libraries that are out there. Some of the benefits that you are going to enjoy the most will include:

- There are some data frames or data structures that are going to be high level compared to some of the others that you can use.
- There is going to be a streamlined process in place to handle the tabular data, and then there is also a functionality that is rich for the time series that you want to work with.

- There is going to be the benefit of data alignment, missing data-friendly statistics, merge, join, and groupby methods to help you handle the data that you have.
- You are able to use the variety of structures for data in Pandas, and you will be able to freely draw on the functions that are present in SciPy and NumPy to help make sure manipulation and other work can be done the way that you want.

Before we move on from here, we also need to have a good look at what some of the types of data are when it comes to Pandas. Pandas is going to be well suited when it comes to a large amount of data and will be able to help you sort through almost any kind of data that you would like. Some of the data types that are going to be the most suitable for working with the Pandas library with Python will include:

- Any kind of tabular data that is going to have columns that are heterogeneously typed.
- Arbitrary matrix data that has labels for the columns and rows.
- Unordered and ordered time-series data

- Any other kinds of sets of data that are statistical and observational.

Working with the Pandas library is one of the best ways to handle some of the Python codings that you want to do with the help of data analysis. As a company, it is so important to be able to go through and not just collect data, but also to be able to read through that information and learn some of the trends and the information that is available there. being able to do this can provide your company with some of the insights that it needs to do better, and really grow while providing customer service.

There are a lot of different methods that you can use when it comes to performing data analysis. And some of them are going to work in a different way than we may see with Python or with the Pandas library. But when it comes to efficiently and quickly working through a lot of data, and having a multitude of algorithms and more that can sort through all of this information, working with the Python Pandas is the best option.

-

Chapter 3 Fundamentals of Statistics

Why Statistics is Important for Data Science?

Some of the algorithms in machine learning have been borrowed from statistics. So, we need some basic knowledge of statistics to understand how to extract useful information from data and how to build estimation models for data prediction based on hypothesis and assumptions. For example, linear regression is widely used in several machine learning problems. In statistics, it is used for fitting a line to data values while in machine learning, it is more like learning weights (constant values in line equation) through examples.

Some uses of statistics in machine learning are:

• Data Understanding: *Understanding distribution of data variables and their relationships. So, we can design a model predictor best suited for data. For this, we need to understand what data distribution is, what relationships our variables can have and how to understand those relationships.*

- Data Cleaning: *We cannot simply get raw data and feed it to machine learning models for our task. There are certain complexities within. For example, the data might be corrupted, erroneous or just missing. So, we need to fix those issues e.g. we can fill the missing data following the same data distribution, we can identify outliers and abnormal data distributions to eliminate corruption or errors.*

- *Data Preparation*: Sometimes, our data features are not all on the same scale which leads to some issues in model training (It is further explained in training models part). Sometimes, the data is textual and we need to encode it in numeric form to make it compatible for our model. So we need data scaling, sampling and encoding from statistics.

- Model Configuration and Selection: *Hyperparameters of a machine learning model control the learning method which can lead to different results from the model. Using statistical hypothesis testing technique from statistics, we can compare results of different hyperparameters. Similarly, we need such statistical techniques to select a model by comparing models' results and their properties.*

• Model Evaluation: *To evaluate a model, we need statistical methods for data sampling and resampling. We also need metrics to properly evaluate model and quantify the variability in predictions using estimation statistics.*

Data Types

Data in statistics is classified in following types and subtypes:

4) Qualitative Data
      a. Nominal/Categorical
      b. Ordinal
5) Quantitative Data
      a. Discrete
      b. Continuous
         i.   Interval
         ii. Ratio

Qualitative Data

Qualitative data is non-numerical and categorical data. Categorical data can be counted, grouped and ranked in order of importance. Such data is grouped to bring order or make sense of the data.

Nominal:

Nominal scales represent data that does not have quantitative values or any numerical significance. This scale is used for classification or categorization of the variables. These variables are simply labels of data without any specific order. Such scale is often used in surveys and questionnaires.

Of these three colors, which one do you like the most?

6) Red
7) Green
8) Blue

For example, in the above question, color is a categorical variable but there is no specific way to order these colors from low to high or high to low.

So, for a question in a survey:

Which pizza crust do you like?

5) Thin Crust
6) Stuffed Crust

7) Cheese Stuffed Crust

8) Hand Tossed Crust

Only the types of crust are significant of analysis and their order does not matter. The results of such questions are analyzed to provide the most common answer which describes the customers' preferences.

ORDINAL:

Ordinal scale represents data that has some specific order. That order relates elements of data to each other in a ranked fashion. Numbers can be assigned as labels and are not mathematically measured as scales.

How satisfied you are with your test scores:

Chapter 17 Extremely Unsatisfied

Chapter 18 Unsatisfied

Chapter 19 Neutral

Chapter 20 Satisfied

Chapter 21 Extremely Satisfied

Here, these options are assigned numbers, that is, a ranking of 5 is better than a ranking of 3 but we cannot quantify the difference between these two rankings (i.e. how good ranking 5 is compared to ranking 3).

Quantitative Data

Data that is numerical or can be measured is called quantitative data. For example, heights of 12 years old boys, GPA of a class, Distance of stars, Temperature of the day and so on. Numerical data have two sub data types:

5) Discrete
6) Continuous

DISCRETE:

Discrete data is numerical data that can not be subdivided into smaller parts. For example, number of people in a room, number of apples in a basket, number of planets in solar system, etc.

CONTINUOUS:

Continuous data can be broken down into smaller parts. For example, temperature, distance, weight of a person, etc. Continuous data can be further categorized into two types:

5) Interval
6) Ratio

Interval:

Interval scale represents data that has specific order and that order has mathematical significance, which means that unlike nominal and ordinal scales, the interval scale quantifies the difference between the order of variables. This scale is quite effective because we can apply statistical analysis on such data. The only drawback of this scale is that we cannot compute ratios because it does not have a true zero value (a starting point for values) and hence, a zero value does not mean "absence of value" and is therefore not meaningful.

For example, 70 degree Celcius is less than 90 degree Celcius and their difference is a measurable 20 C as is the difference between 90 C and 110 C. Also, 40 degree Celcius is not twice as hot as 20 degree Celcius. A value of 0 C is arbitrary as it does not mean "no temperature" and because negative values of temperature do exist.

Ratio:

Ratio scale has all the properties from Interval scale and also defines a true zero value. A meaningful zero in ratio scale means "absence of value". Because of the existence of a true zero value, variables of ratio scale does not have negative values and it allows to measure ratio between two variables. This scale allows to apply techniques of inferential and descriptive statistics to variables. Some examples of ratio variables are height, weight, money, age and time.

For example, what is your weight in pounds?

- *< 100 lbs*

- *100 lbs - 120 lbs*

- *121 lbs - 140 lbs*

- *141 lbs - 160 lbs*

- *> 160 lbs*

Similarly, there is no such thing as age 0, because that essentially means you don't exist. Because of this, we can compare that an age of 24 is twice the age of 12 and that we cannot have negative age value.

Statistics in Practice

Statistics is defined as the collection, analysis and interpretation of data. It transforms raw data to useful information and helps us understand our data required to train our machine learning models and interpret their results. The field of statistics has two major divisions: Descriptive statistics and Inferential statistics. Both of these divisions combined are powerful tools for data understanding, description and data prediction. Descriptive statistics describes and interprets data and helps us understand how two variables or processes are related while inferential statistics is used to reason from available data.

Descriptive Statistics

Descriptive statistics describes features of data by summarizing it. For example we have test scores of 100 students from a class. Descriptive statistics gives detailed information about those scores e.g. how spread the scores are, if there are outliers (scores way above or lower than average score), how scores are distributed (how many students with low score, high score or average score) and many other similar stats of those results.

Basic Definitions

POPULATION

Population is something under observation for study. It is a set of observations. It also describes the subject of a particular study. For example, if we are studying weights of men, the population would be the set of weights of all men of the world.

Population Parameters

Population parameters are characteristics and stats about population such as mean, standard deviation.

Sample

Sample is a randomly taken small part of the population or just a subset of the population. The observations and conclusions made on sample data represent properties or attributes of the entire population. For example, consider a study where we want to know how many hours, on average, do a teenager spends in physical exercise. Since, surveying all the teenagers of the world or even a country is impractical because of time and resource constraint. So, we take a sample from the population that represents the entire population.

Descriptive statistics is further divided into measures of center and measures of dispersion.

3) Measures of Center
 a. Mean
 b. Median
 c. Mode

4) Measures of Dispersion
 a. Range
 b. Percentiles/Quartiles
 c. Interquartile range
 d. Variance
 e. Standard Deviation
 f. Kurtosis
 g. Skewness

Measure of Center/Central Tendency

Central tendency describes a dataset with a single value which is the central position within that dataset. This central position provides summary of the whole data.

Three measures of central tendency are:

- Mean

- Median

- Mode

Mean

It refers to the mean or average of data and is the sum of all values of the data divided by the number of values. It is represented by letter μ or x and is given by:

$$\mu = \frac{1}{n}\sum_{i=1}^{n} x_i$$

Some properties of mean make it very useful for measuring

For example, consider following array of numbers and their mean calculated:

Given Array: $\{-5, 6, 3, 0, 6\}$

$$\mu = \frac{(-5 + 6 + 3 + 0 + 6)}{5} = \frac{10}{5}$$

$$\mu = 2.0$$

A disadvantage of using statistical mean is that it can be biased because it is affected by outliers in the data. Consider the above example again and see how the existence of an outlier will affect the mean value:

Given Array: { – 5, 6, 3, 0, 6, 110 }

$$\mu = \frac{(-5 + 6 + 3 + 0 + 6 + 110)}{6} = \frac{120}{6}$$

$\mu = 20.0$

Median

Median is another measure of central tendency and is the middle value of ascendingly sorted data. If the number of values in dataset is even, the median is the mean value of two middle values in sorted array.

Given Array { – 5, 6, 3, 0, 6 }

Sorted in Ascending Order { – 5, 0, 3, 6, 6 }

Median is our middle value in sorted array = 3

One important property of median is that it is not affected by outliers. Consider the example of statistical mean with outlier:

Given Array { – 5, 6, 3, 0, 6, 110 }

Sorted in Ascending Order { – 5, 0, 3, 6, 6, 110 }

$$\text{Median} = \frac{(3 + 6)}{2} = \frac{9}{2}$$

$$\text{Median} = 4.5$$

So, median should be used when data is skewed (not symmetric).

Mode

Mode is the most frequently occurring value in the data. Some datasets can be multimodal (having more than one modes) and some may not have any mode at all. For example,

Given Array $\{1, 6, 0, 9, 3, -2, 4, -1, -1, 5, 1, 5, 3, 1, 7, -3, -4, 7, 8, -1\}$

Modes: $-1, 1$

Given Array: $\{-1, 7, 3, 15, 2\}$

This data does not have any mode

Mode is rarely used as central measure of tendency. One problem with mode is that there can be multiple modes in data and they can be spread out.

Following three histograms with different symmetric and skewed distributions show three

190

measures of center. In case of symmetric (normal) distribution, mean, median and mode are all same. Although we can use any of these three measures but mean is usually preferred because it considers all the values of data in calculation, which is not the case for median and mode.

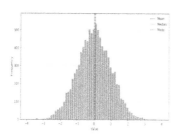

Now consider when the data is right skewed. Here, mean is not a good representation of the center of dataset and so, we can better choose median measure.

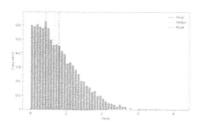

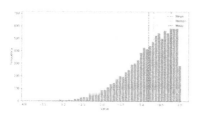

Measures of Dispersion

Measure of dispersion tells how much the data distribution is stretched out or how variable the data is. Sometimes, measure of central tendency is not enough to grasp the distribution of data. For example, two data distributions can have same mean but one distribution can be more spread out than the other.

Range

It is the simplest measure of dispersion. It is the difference between the maximum value and the minimum value of the data.

Given Array: $\{-4, 7, 1, 7, -5, 6, 3, 0\}$

Range: $7 - (-5) = 12$

Range provides us a quick way to get a rough idea of the spread of distribution but it does not give much detail about the data. Two datasets can have same range but their values can vary significantly. Also, range is sensitive to outliers or extreme values.

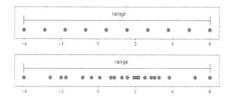

Percentile

A percentile represents a value below which a given percentage of data falls. In other words, percentile is the relative position of a value in sorted dataset. A student scored 89 out of 100 in a test. This figure alone does not have significant meaning unless we know what was his/her position in class. May be, a score of 89 falls in the 30th percentile which means that it is better than 30% of the class or may be 70th percentile (70% of students have scored less than 89 on test).

Index of a number at P_{th} percentile in an ordered list of values is given by:

$$Index = \frac{P}{100} * N$$

For example,

Given Sorted Values: { − 1,5,12,13,30,50}

For example, for list of numbers given above,

15th percentile : P_{15}
$$= \frac{15}{100} * 6 = 0.9 \approx 1 \ (1st \ number \ in \ the \ list$$
)

30th percentile : P_{30}
$$= \frac{30}{100} * 6 = 1.8 \approx 2 \ (2nd \ number \ in \ the \ list$$
)

60th percentile : P_{60}
$$= \frac{60}{100} * 6 = 3.6 \approx 4 \ (4th \ number \ in \ the \ list$$
)

99th percentile : P_{99}
$$= \frac{99}{100} * 6 = 5.9 \approx 6 \ (6th \ number \ in \ the \ list$$
)

Quartiles

Quartiles are three values that divide a dataset into 4 parts where each part contains 25% of the total data. First, second and third quartiles are actually 25th, 50th and 75th percentiles respectively. First quartile divides the data in 1:3 parts and has 25% of data on the left side(or below it). Second quartile divides the data in 1:1 while the third quartile divides the data in 3:1 parts (75% data on left side). So, second quartile is actually the middle value (or median) of the dataset and it divides the data into two equal parts. Then, first quartile is the middle value (or median) of the first part and third quartile is the middle value (or median) of the second part.

For example,

Given array:

[10, − 9, − 7, 10, 3, − 10, − 2, − 3, 14, − 2, − 6, − 9, 14, 16, 0]

Sorted array:

[− 10, − 9, − 9, − 7, − 6, − 3, − 2, − 2, 0, 3, 10, 10, 14, 14, 16]

$Q_1 = -2$

InterQuartile Range

Interquartile range (IRQ) is the difference between third quartile and first quartile. An important property of IQR is that it is not affected by outlier values, which makes it preferable over range. It focuses on the middle 50% values of data.

Sorted array:

$[-10, -9, -9, -7, -6, -3, -2, -2, 0, 3, 10, 10, 14, 14, 16]$

IRQ: 16.5

Visual representation of some of these measures is shown in following boxplot.

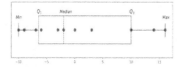

Variance

It is a measure of the spread of data. It quantifies how far, on average, the data is from the mean value.

$$Var(X) = \frac{1}{N}\sum_{i=1}^{N}(x_i - \mu)^2$$

Standard Deviation

Standard deviation is just the square root of variance. The difference between variance and standard deviation is that variance value is on a large scale while standard deviation has the same scale as other dataset values. It is represented by the greek letter σ and is given by:

$$\sigma = \sqrt{Var(X)}$$

For example, consider following values, their mean and standard deviation has been calculated:

{2, 8, 0, 2, −2, −4, 7, 1, 7 = 5 6 7, 0, 6, 0, 6, 0, 6,   5, 3}

$\mu = 2.95$

$\sigma = 4.2$

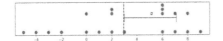

Skewness

Skewness is a measure of data asymmetry. A symmetric distribution means that the data values are equally distributed around the mean value, as in the case of a normal distribution. In case of asymmetry, data is distributed unevenly or the distribution is not symmetrical about the mean. In positively skewed data distribution, values are concentrated to the left and in negatively skewed data, values are concentrated to the right as shown in figure below. If data skewness is not close to zero, the data is not normally distributed.

$$Skewness = \frac{\frac{1}{N}\sum_{i=1}^{N}(x_i - \mu)^3}{\sigma^3}$$

Kurtosis

Kurtosis describes the tail of a distribution with reference to a normal distribution. A normal distribution has a kurtosis equal to 3 and is called mesokurtic. A distribution with shorter and thinner tails, broader and lower peaks than a normal distribution is called platykurtic and has kurtosis less than 3. A distribution with longer tails, higher and sharper peaks than a normal distribution is called leptykurtic and has kurtosis greater than 3.

$$Kurtosis = \frac{\frac{1}{N}\sum_{i=1}^{N}(x_i - \mu)^4}{\sigma^4}$$

Where N is the number of values, μ is mean of values and σ is standard deviation.

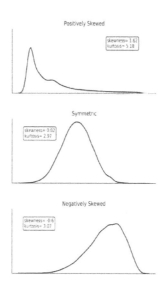

Chapter 4 Visualization and results

In the previous chapters we learnt how to handle data. In this chapter we are going to learn methods of visualizing data as well as creating figures to present analysis of data. In order to develop figures, many libraries are available in Python. This section presents only functionalities of the matplolib library which is an advanced library in Python to develop figures.

Matplotlib library in Python

Matplolib library is an open source advanced package available in Python for data visualization. Data visualization is crucial in data analysis as well as to communicate the results to stakeholders. This library is based on the NumPy library too. One module of matplotlib library that is very used is the Pyplot. This module has similar interface as Matlab a programming tool that is efficient for numerical programming. If you did not install matplotlib yet, you can do so by typing the following command in python prompt:

pip install matplotlib

If you have installed Anaconda and you are using Jupyter, this library should be already installed by default. All you have to do is import the package.

Before dining into examples and how to use the matplotlib library, let's see the component of a figure that we can set. A figure is entire figure that is formed by one or more axes which are called a plot. Axes is what is commonly named as a plot. A figure can be formed by different axes depending on the type of plotting we are making 1D, 2D or 3D. Axis are responsible of setting the limits of a plot. Artist is all the components that can be in a figure like a text object, collection objects.

Basic plot in matplotlib

We will start first in this chapter by the Pyplot module in matplotlib. This module offers the basic functions to supplement components to the current axes of a figure. To use this module, it should be imported as follows:

>>> import numpy as np

>>> import matplotlib.pyplot as plt

Note here we imported the Numpy library as well because we will be working with numpy arrays.

Now we can create a single plot of a data using the function plot(). Let's create a series of data and plot these data.

```
>>> X = np.array([1,2,3,4])
>>> Y = X ** 2
>>> plt.plot(X,Y)
>>> plt.show()
```

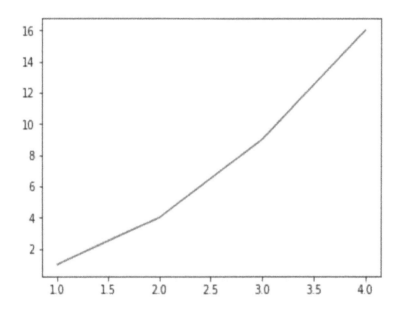

In this example, we created an array of values and computed the square of each value. The plot function is supplied with 2 inputs where the 1st argument is values of X-axis and the 2nd argument is corresponding values of Y-axis. Now it would be helpful to understand the plotting if we had a legend of the axis and a title for the plot. To add these elements into our plotting, we can use the *xlabel()* function that adds a label to the x-axis and *ylabel()* function that adds a label to the y-axis. The *title()* function adds a title to the plot.

```
>>> A = np.array([1,2,3,4])
>>> B = A ** 2
>>> plt.plot(A,B)
>>> plt.xlabel('A labels')
>>> plt.ylabel('B= A**2')
>>> plt.title('My first in Python')
>>> plt.show()
```

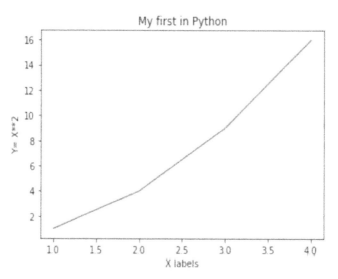

Now we can change the size of the figure using the figure function and passing argument that specifies the size of the figure. For example, let's change the size of the previous figure we created.

```
>>> A = np.array([1,2,3,4])
>>> B = A ** 2
>>> plt.figure(figsize=(5,5))
>>> plt.plot(A,B)
>>> plt.xlabel('A labels')
>>> plt.ylabel('B= A**2')
>>> plt.title('My first in Python with different size')
>>> plt.show()
```

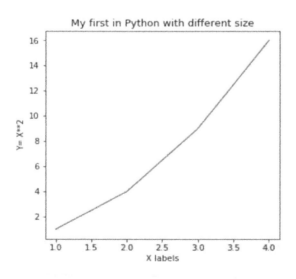

The plot function can take other input argument. In fact, we can plot two different datasets in the same plot. Let's define compute the values of X ** 3 and plot it in the same figure as an example.

>>> A = np.array([1,2,3,4])

>>> B = A ** 2

>>> B2 = A ** 3

>>> plt.figure(figsize=(10,5))

>>> plt.plot(A,B, A,B2)

>>> plt.xlabel('A labels')

>>> plt.ylabel('B= A**2')

>>> plt.title('My first in Python with two dataset')

>>> plt.show()

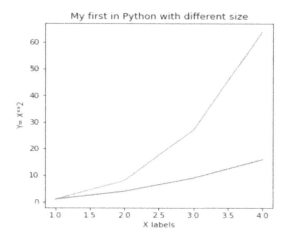

Note that by default the plot function used a different color to plot the second dataset. Also, by default plot function draws the data as a line. In fact, we can pass another argument to the plot function that will specify how the data is plot. In other words, we specify if data is plotted as a line or using another marker such '+', '*', '0'. We can also specify the color. For instance, 'go' will make the plot function to use o to plot the data and the data will be plotted in green. We can also specify the line width if the data is plotted as a line. For example:

```
>>> A = np.array([1,2,3,4])
>>> B=A ** 2
>>> B2 = A ** 3
>>> plt.figure(figsize=(10,5))
>>> plt.plot(A,B,A,B2,linewidth=5)
>>> plt.xlabel('A labels')
>>> plt.ylabel('B= A**2')
>>> plt.title('My first in Python with two datasets and Line width=5')
>>> plt.show()
```

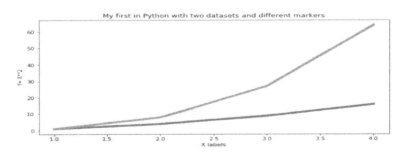

The following example uses different markers to plot two datasets:

>>> X = np.array([1,2,3,4])

>>> Y = X ** 2

>>> Y2 = X ** 3

>>> plt.figure(figsize=(5,5))

>>> plt.plot(X,Y,'r*', X,Y2, 'ko')

>>> plt.xlabel('X labels')

>>> plt.ylabel('Y= X**2')

>>> plt.title('My first in Python with two datasets and different markers')

>>> plt.show()

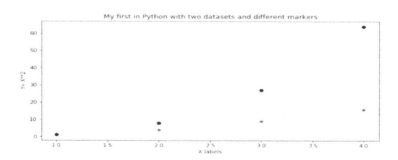

Multiple plots in same figure

You plot several plots in the same figure using the *subplot()* function. Note the datasets that we

207

plotted in the previous section in the same plot can be plotted in different plots in the same figure. The *subplot()* function takes as inputs the following arguments ncols, nrows and finally index. The ncols indicate the number of columns in the figure, nrows the numbers of rows in the figure and the index point toward which plot. For example, we can plot our two datasets in a figure with two rows as follows:

```
>>> X = np.array([1,2,3,4])
>>> Y = X ** 2
>>> Y2 = X ** 3
>>> plt.figure(figsize=(10,10))
>>> plt.subplot(2,1,1)
>>> plt.plot(X,Y,linewidth=5)
>>> plt.xlabel('X labels')
>>> plt.ylabel('Y= X**2')
>>> plt.title('My first subplot in Python')
>>> plt.subplot(2,1,2)
>>> plt.plot(X,Y2,linewidth=5)
>>> plt.xlabel('X labels')
>>> plt.ylabel('Y= X**3')
>>> plt.title('My second subplot in Python')
```

```
>>> plt.show()
```

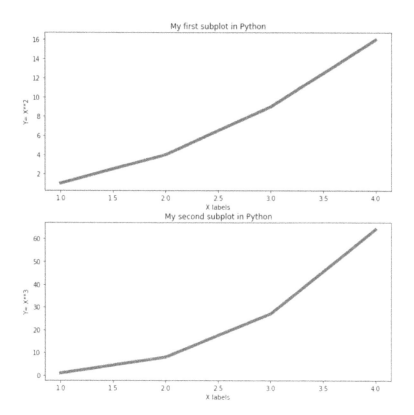

We can plot the two data set in a figure with two columns and two rows by passing as argument to the subplot (1,2,1) and (1,2,2) as follows:

```
>>> X = np.array([1,2,3,4])

>>> Y = X ** 2

>>> Y2 = X ** 3

>>> plt.figure(figsize=(10,10))
```

```
>>> plt.subplot(1,2,1)

>>> plt.plot(X,Y,linewidth=5)

>>> plt.xlabel('X labels')

>>> plt.ylabel('Y= X**2')

>>> plt.title('My first subplot in Python')

>>> plt.subplot(1,2,2)

>>> plt.plot(X,Y2,linewidth=5)

>>> plt.xlabel('X labels')

>>> plt.ylabel('Y= X**3')

>>> plt.title('My second subplot in Python')

>>> plt.show()
```

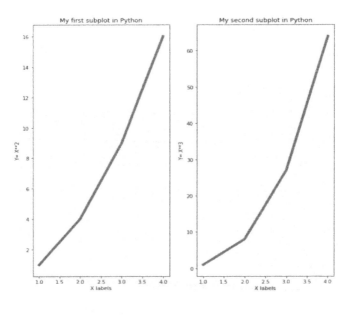

Type of plots

The matplotlib offers several functions to create different graphs that are useful in data science and statistical analysis. The bar graphs are a handy graph to assess and compare different groups among data and explore their distribution. The *bar()* function take as input argument a set of categorial data and their associated values. It takes also optionally a color if you want to make a bar graph where each category is represented with a specific color. For example, let's take the Iris data from the example in the previous chapter about Data frame data structure. Remember the Iris data is formed by a by a sample of 3 species of the Iris flower. Each species is described by sepals and petals length and sepals and petals width. This dataset is available in the sklearn library from which we are going to import the dataset. Because we will be using DataFrame structure we will import the Pandas library as well and we are going to create a Dataframe for the Iris dataset.

>>> import pandas as pd

>>> import numpy as np

>>> from sklearn import datasets

>>> Iris = datasets.load_iris()

I>>> Iris_d = Iris.data

>>> Iris_DF = pd.DataFrame(Iris_d, columns=Iris.feature_names)

The Iris data set has also a variable associated with each value of the sepal length and width as well as lengths and width of the petal. This variable indicates the Iris follower's species and is stored in the variable target. In the following command we are going to create a variable for this variable target:

>>> Y = Iris.target

Now that we have our data ready, we are going to plot a bar graph of the sepal length as follows:

>>> plt.bar(Y, Iris_DF['sepal length (cm)'])

>>> plt.title(' Bar Graph of the Sepal length')

>>> plt.xlabel(' Iris Species')

>>> plt.ylabel(' Count')

>>> plt.show()

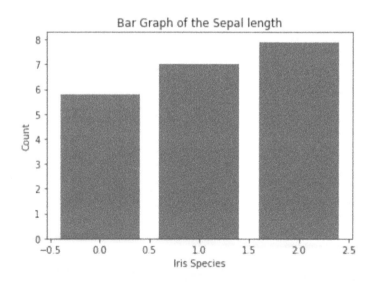

By default, Python plot figures in blue. We can change the color of the bars in the graph by passing the argument color as follows:

>>> plt.bar(Y, Iris_DF['sepal length (cm)'], color='black')

>>> plt.title(' Bar Graph of the Sepal length')

>>> plt.xlabel(' Iris Species')

>>> plt.ylabel(' Count')

>>> plt.show()

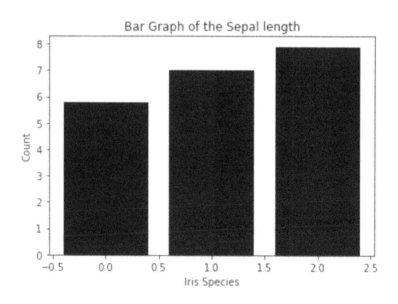

We can also change the orientation of the bars from vertical bars to horizontal bars using the function *barh()*. The barh() function takes the same input argument as the *bar()* function. Let's plot horizontal bar graph for the sepal width length for each Iris species.

>>> plt.barh(Y,Iris_DF['sepal length (cm)'], color='black')

>>> plt.title(' Bar Graph of the Sepal length')

>>> plt.xlabel(' Iris Species')

>>> plt.ylabel(' Count')

>>> plt.show()

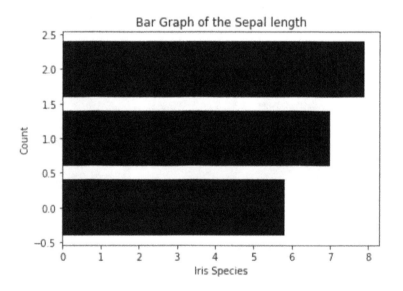

We can also supply the *bar()* or the *barh()* function with an extra argument xerr or yerr(if using the *bar()* function) and its values. For example, if we want o plot also the variance of the variable for which the bar graph is plotted. For example, in the case of the sepal length we can do if we are using *barh()* function:

>>> # Computing the variance with Numpy library

>>> V = np.var(Iris_DF['sepal length (cm)'])

>>> plt.barh(Y, Iris_DF['sepal length (cm)'], xerr = V, color = 'grey')

>>> plt.title(' Bar Graph of the Sepal length with Variance')

>>> plt.xlabel(' Iris Species')

>>> plt.ylabel(' Count')

>>> plt.show()

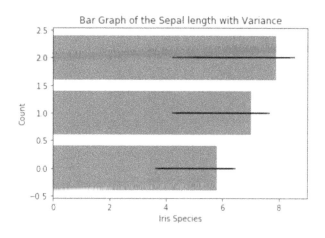

If the function *bar()* is used for vertical bars, to plot the variance with bars we pass as argument yerr as follows:

>>> plt.bar(Y, Iris_DF['sepal length (cm)'], yerr = V, color = 'grey')

>>> plt.title(' Bar Graph of the Sepal length with Variance')

>>> plt.xlabel(' Iris Species')

>>> plt.ylabel(' Count')

>>> plt.show()

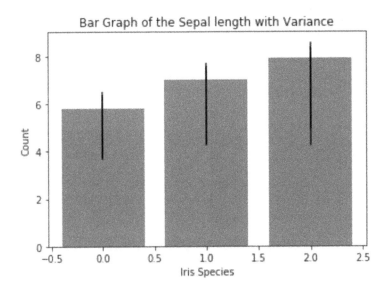

Sometimes, we have a dataset with multiple variables and we want to create a single bar graph that shows the bars for different variables for each category like in the case of the Iris data set we are using in this chapter. To plot or stack multiple bars in the same graph, we need to use the *bar()* function as many times as the number of the variables for which the graph are plotted. In this case, we need to specify the index and width for the bars to stack them together. Let's see how we can use this in order to plot in the same graph sepal length and sepal width bars. First, we need to group the Iris flowers according to the species and compute the mean sepal length and mean sepal width for each species. Remember we can do that using the *groupby()* function like we did in the previous chapter. We also need to add the Y variable which indicates the Iris species into our DataFrame.

>>> data = Iris_DF

>>> data['Y'] = Y # Adding the Y variable to the Dataframe

>>> grouped_data = data.groupby(' Y ') # Grouping the Iris flowers according to the species

>>> # Computing the mean sepal length and width for each species

>>> M = grouped_data['sepal length (cm)'].agg(np.mean)

```
>>> M2 = grouped_data['sepal width
(cm)'].agg(np.mean)
```

```
>>> print(' The mean sepal length (cm) for
each species is:', M)
```

The mean sepal length (cm) for each
species is: Y
0   5.006
1   5.936
2   6.588
Name: sepal length (cm), dtype: float64
```
>>> print(' The mean width (cm) of the sepal
for each species is:', M)
```

The mean sepal width (cm) for each species is: Y

0   5.006

1 5.936

2 6.588

Name: sepal length (cm), dtype: float64

Now that the data is ready, we plot the stacked bar graph as follows:

```
>>> ind = np.arange(3)
```

```
>>> width = 0.3

>>> plt.bar (ind, M, width, color = 'grey')

>>> plt.bar (ind + width, M2, width, color = 'blue')

>>> plt.title(' Bar Graph of the Sepal length
and width (cm)')

>>> plt.xlabel(' Iris Species')

>>> plt.ylabel(' Count')

>>> plt.show()
```

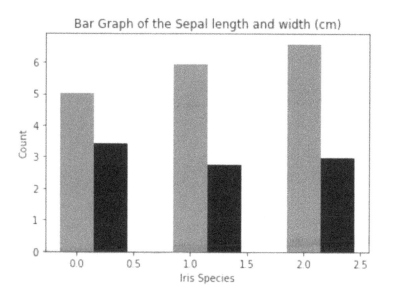

We can add a legend to our graph using the *legend()*
function in oder to distinguish between the graphs.
We can also define specify in the graph the position
of ticks in axis. The following statements how we can
do that:

```
>>> ind = np.arange(3)

>>> width = 0.3

>>> plt.bar (ind, M, width, color = 'grey',
label = 'Sepal length(cm)')

>>> plt.bar (ind + width, M2, width, color =
'blue', label = 'Sepal width(cm)')

>>> plt.title(' Bar Graph of the Sepal length
and width (cm)')

>>> plt.xlabel(' Iris Species')

>>> plt.ylabel(' Count')

>>> plt.xticks(ind + width/2, ind) # Position
of the xticks

>>> plt.legend(loc = 'best') # Position of the
legend

>>> plt.show()
```

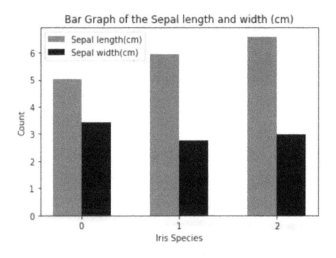

We can also stack the bars vertically. In this case we pass an argument to the *bar()* function fro the second variable and specify the bar graph of the values below. For example, to stack vertically the sepal lenght and width we follow the code presented in below:

```
>>> ind = np.arange(3)

>>> width = 0.3

>>> plt.bar (ind, M, width, color = 'grey', label = 'Sepal length(cm)')

>>> plt.bar (ind, M2, width, color = 'blue', label = 'Sepal width(cm)', bottom = M)

>>> plt.title(' Bar Graph of the Sepal length and width (cm)')

>>> plt.xlabel(' Iris Species')

>>> plt.ylabel(' Count')

>>> plt.xticks(ind + width/2, ind) # Position of the xticks

>>> plt.legend(loc = 'best') # Position of the legend

>>> plt.show()
```

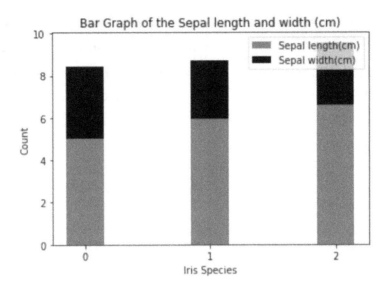

Bar Graph of the Sepal length and width (cm)

Histograms are another common graph in data analysis and statistical analysis that show the distribution of a variable. The histogram is a plot that shows the frequency of the values that a variable can take. In other words, we plot the range values of a variable against its frequency which describe the distribution of the variable. The *hist()* function allows to plot histograms with matplotlib library. For example, let's plot the histogram of the sepal length of the Iris data:

>>> plt.title(' Histogram of the Iris sepal length')

>>> plt.xlabel ('Sepal length (cm)')

>>> plt.ylabel (' Frequency')

>>> plt.hist(Iris_DF['sepal length (cm)'])

```
>>> plt.show()
```

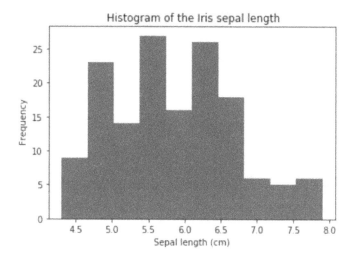

Like the other plot functions, color of the histogram can be changed by passing a color input argument like in the following example:

```
>>> plt.title(' Histogram of the Iris sepal length')
```

```
>>> plt.xlabel ('Sepal length (cm)')
```

```
>>> plt.ylabel (' Frequency')
```

```
>>> plt.hist(Iris_DF['sepal length (cm)'], color = 'grey')
```

```
>>> plt.show()
```

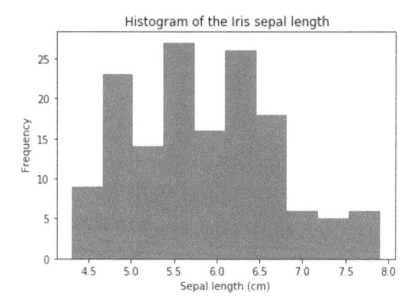

Histogram of the Iris sepal length

In order to detect visually correlation between the variables we can use scatter plots that plots variables against each other in 2-dimensional space. To plot a scatter plot, we use the function *scatter()*. For example, we plot the sepal length against the sepal width:

```
>>> plt.scatter(Iris_DF['sepal length (cm)'],
Iris_DF['sepal width (cm)'])
```

```
>>> plt.title( ' Scatter plot of sepal length and
sepal width')
```

```
>>> plt.xlabel(' Sepal length (cm)')
```

```
>>> plt.ylabel (' Sepal width (cm)')
```

```
>>> plt.show()
```

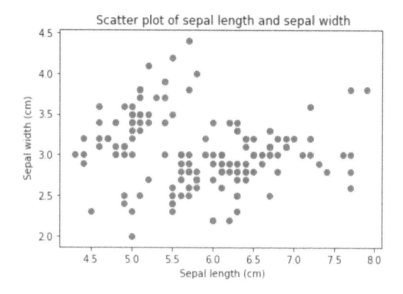

Scatter plot of sepal length and sepal width

The scatter plot in the figure above is in a 2-dimensional space. We can also visualize the same scatter in a 3-dimensional space using *scatter3D()* function. This function is part of the mplot3d for 3 dimensional plots. So, we import first the module than plot the scatter plot in a 3-dimensional plot as follows:

>>> from mpl_toolkits import mplot3d

>>> ax = plt.axes(projection='3d')

>>> ax.scatter3D (Iris_DF['sepal length (cm)'], Iris_DF['sepal width (cm)'])

>>> ax.set_xlabel(' Sepal length (cm)')

```
>>> ax.set_ylabel (' Sepal width (cm)')
```

```
>>> ax.set_title(' 3-D scatter plot of sepal
length and sepal width')
```

```
>>> plt.show()
```

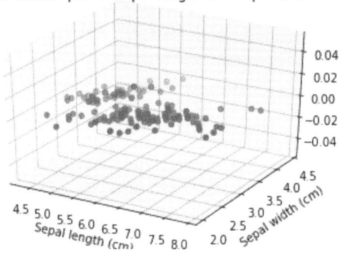

Chapter 5 Writing Loops in Python

The next thing that we need to take a look at when it is time to write some of your own codes in Python will be looped. Creating loops can help you to make a code that is more efficient, and will ensure that you are able to get codes written quickly and without a ton of work in the process. These loops work well with some of the conditional statements that we are going to talk about, later on, helping you to clear up your code while getting a lot done in a short amount of time.

Loops are helpful because they are going to speed up how long it is going to take you to write out some codes, can help to clean it all up, and can take hundreds of lines of code (potentially), and put it in just a few lines if needed. Think about how much time that is going to save when you can get all of that code into a few lines with the help of the loops.

If you are working on your code and you find that there are parts of the program that can repeat them over and over again, at least a few times, then the loops are going to help make this happen. You will be able to get the code to repeat as many times as you would like, without having to rewrite the same codes over and over again.

Let's say that you would like to work on some kind of program that has a multiplication table that is going to go from 1 to 10 and all of the answers that are needed for it. Maybe you would choose to do some of the beginner codes and write it all line by line while wasting a ton of time and making it so that the code looks kind of messy in the process. But you are able to use the idea of a lop and write it out with the help of a few lines. We will explore some of the different options that are available for the loops and using them, while also seeing how you would be able to do the example above in just a few lines.

While this may seem like a complex thing to work within the coding, it is actually pretty easy to work with, and even a beginner is going to be able to write out some of these codes. The way that these codes will work is that it tells the compiler to keep reading the same part of the code until there is some condition that is met. Once that condition is met, the compiler will get out of the loop and start working on the next part of the code.

So, let's say that you are working on a program, and a part of it needs to be able to count from one to ten. You would be able to use the idea of the loop in order to tell the compiler to keep going through the code until it reaches higher than ten. We can take a look at a few of the different examples that you are able to do with the ideas of the loop.

One thing to remember here is that when you write out some of these loops, it is important to set up the conditions in the right manner. It is easy to forget to set up these conditions when you first get started, but if you forget them right from the beginning of the code, then you will end up in a loop that is not going to stop. You will get stuck in a continuous loop because the code doesn't know when it needs to stop going through the loop.

When you decide to work with some of the methods that are considered more traditional with coding, or using some of the other methods that are found throughout this guidebook, your whole goal here will be to write out all of the lines of code to get things done. Even if you see some parts of the code repeating, then you would still need to rewrite it out. This could take a long time and may not be as easy to work with as well. But when you work with loops, this is not going to be something that is going to be that big of a deal.

When working with these loops, you are able to get rid of some of the traditional ways of coding and change it up and make things easier. You will be able to combine together a ton of lines of code, or as many as you would need in order to get things done. The compiler will still be able to read through it when the loop is done in the proper way, just as long as you make sure that all of your conditions are put in place.

Now that we have spent some time looking at what the loops mean and why they are going to be so important to your code writing, it is time to divide up some of the different types of loops that are available to help you get this done inside the codes you write.

The first loop: the while loop
> So, the first type of loop that we are going to explore is the idea of the while loop in Python. This loop is a good one to bring out and use when you want to make sure that your code is able to go through the loop or the cycle for a predetermined number of

times. You can pick out how many times you would like the code to go through this kind of loop to get the best results out of it. This makes it easy to get the number of times you would like the loop to go through.

When you work with the while loop, the goal is not to make the code that you write go through the cycle an indefinite amount of times. But you do have in mind a number of times that you would like the code to do its work. So, if you want to count from one to ten in the code, your goal is to use the while loop in order to go through the loop that many times.

With the while loop, you will see that the code is going to go through the loop, and then it will double check to see if the conditions are met or not. Then, if the conditions are not met, they will go through the loop again and then check again. It will continue doing this over and over again until it has met the conditions, and then it will go on to the other part of the code when the loop is all gone.

To see how the while loop is going to work, and to gain a better understanding of the loop works in general, let's look at some examples of a code that has a while loop inside of it:

```
counter = 1

while(counter <= 3):

principal = int(input("Enter the principal amount:"))

numberofyeras = int(input("Enter the number of
years:"))

rateofinterest = float(input("Enter the rate of
interest:"))

simpleinterest = principal * numberofyears *
rateofinterest/100

print("Simple interest = %.2f" %simpleinterest)

#increase the counter by 1

counter = counter + 1

print("You have calculated simple interest for 3
times!")
```

Before we take a look at some of the other types of
loops that we are able to work with, let's open up
the compiler on Python and type in the code to see
what is going to happen when we execute it. You will
then be able to see how the while loop is able to
work. The program is able to go through and figure
out the interest rates, along with the final amounts

that are associated with it, based on the numbers that the user, or you, will put into the system.

With the example from the code that was above, we have the loop set up so that it is going to go through three times. This means that the user gets a chance to put in different numbers and see the results three times, and then the system will be able to move on. You do get the chance to add in more or take out some loops based on what is the best for your needs.

The second loop: the for loop

At this point, we have been able to take a look at the while loop and what it is all going to entail, it is time to take a look at the for loop so that we are able to see how this in order to do more with loops, and how this is going to be different than the while loop overall. When you work with the while loops, you will notice that the code is going to go through a loop a certain number of times. But it is not always going to work for all of the situations where you want to bring in a loop. And the for loop is going to help us to fill in the blanks that the while loop is not able to do.

When you are ready to work with the for loop, you will be able to set up the code in a manner that the user isn't going to be the one who will go into the code and provide the program with the information that it needs. They do not have the control that is needed to stop the loop from running.

Instead of the user being able to hold the control, the for loop is going to be set up so that it will go over the iteration of your choice in the order that you place the items into your code. This information, when the for loop is going to list them out in the exact way that they are listed in the code. The user will not need to input anything for the for loop to work.

A good example of how this is going to work inside your code so that you are able to make it work for your needs will include the following syntax:

```
# Measure some strings:
words = [`apple,' `mango,' `banana,' `orange']
for w in words:
print(w, len(w))
```

When you work with the for loop example that is above, you are able to add it to your compiler and see what happens when it gets executed. When you do this, the four fruits that come out on your screen will show up in the exact order that you have them written out. If you would like to have them show up in a different order, you can do that, but then you need to go back to your code and rewrite them in the right order, or your chosen order. Once you have then written out in the syntax and they are ready to be executed in the code, you can't make any changes to them.

The third loop: the nested loop

The third and final loop that we are going to work within Python is going to be known as the nested loop. You will find that when we look at the nested loop, there are going to be some parts that are similar to what we looked at with the while loop and with the for loop, but it is going to use these topics in a different way. when you decide to work with a nested loop, you will just take one loop, and then make sure that it is placed inside of another loop. Then, both of these loops will work together and continue on with their work until both have had a chance to finish.

This may seem really hard to work with when it comes to the loops, and you may wonder if there is actually any time that you, as a beginner, would need to work with this loop. But there are often a lot more chances to work with the nested loop than you may think in the beginning. For example, if you are working some kind of code that needs to have a multiplication table inside of it, and you want the answers listed all the way up, then you are going to work with the nested loop.

Imagine how long this kind of process is going to take if you have to go out and list each and every part of the code without using a loop to make it happen. You would have to write out the lines of codes to do one time one, one's times two, and so on until you reach the point where you are at ten times ten. This would end up being a ton of lines of code just to make this kind of table work in your code. But you are able to work with the idea of the nested loop in order to see the results that you want.

A good example that you will be able to work with to show how a nested loop works and to make sure that you are able to make a full multiplication table of your own, includes the following:

```
#write a multiplication table from 1 to 10

For x in xrange(1, 11):

For y in xrange(1, 11):

Print '%d = %d' % (x, y, x*x)
```

When you got the output of this program, it is going to look similar to this:

```
1*1 = 1

1*2 = 2

1*3 = 3

1*4 = 4
```

All the way up to 1*10 = 2

Then it would move on to do the table by twos such as this:

```
2*1 =2

2*2 = 4
```

And so on until you end up with 10*10 = 100 as your final spot in the sequence.

Go ahead and put this into the compiler and see what happens. You will simply have four lines of code, and end up with a whole multiplication table that shows up on your program. Think of how many lines of code you would have to write out to get this table the traditional way that you did before? This table only took a few lines to accomplish, which shows how powerful and great the nested loop can be.

As you can see, there are a lot of different things that you are able to do when you start to implement some loops into the codes that you are writing. There are a ton of reasons why you should add a loop into the code you are writing. You will be able to use it in most cases to take a large amount of code and write it in just a few lines instead. This saves you time, cleans up the code that you are trying to light, and the compiler is going to be able to still help you do some things that are super powerful!

Chapter 6 K-Means Clustering

Clustering falls under the category of unsupervised machine learning algorithms. It is often applied when the data is not labeled. The goal of the algorithm is to identify clusters or groups within the data.

The idea behind the clusters is that the objects contained one cluster is more related to one another than the objects in the other clusters. The similarity is a metric reflecting the strength of the relationship between two data objects. Clustering is highly applied in exploratory data mining. In have many uses in diverse fields such as pattern recognition, machine learning, information retrieval, image analysis, data compression, bio-informatics, and computer graphics.

The algorithm forms clusters of data based on the similarity between data values. You are required to specify the value of K, which are the number of clusters that you expect the algorithm to make from the data. The algorithm first selects a centroid value for every cluster. After that, it performs three steps in an iterative manner:

- Calculate the Euclidian distance between every data instance and the centroids for all clusters.
- Assign the instances of data to the cluster of centroid with the nearest distance.
- Calculate the new centroid values depending on the mean values of the coordinates of the data instances from the corresponding cluster.

Let us manually demonstrate how this algorithm works before implementing it on Scikit-Learn:

Suppose we have two dimensional data instances given below and by the name D:

D = { (5,3), (10,15), (15,12), (24,10), (30,45), (85,70), (71,80), (60,78), (55,52), (80,91) }

Our goal is to divide the data into two clusters, namely C1 and C2 depending on the similarity between the data points.

We should first initialize the values for the centroids of both clusters, and this should be done randomly. The centroids will be named C1 and C2 for clusters C1 and C2 respectively, and we will initialize them with the values for the first two data points, that is, (5,3) and (10,15). It is after this that you should begin the iterations.

Anytime that you calculate the Euclidean distance, the data point should be assigned to the cluster with the shortest Euclidean distance. Let us take the example of the data point (5,3):

Euclidean Distance from the Cluster Centroid C1 = (5,3) = 0

Euclidean Distance from the Cluster Centroid C2 = (10,15) = 13

The Euclidean distance for the data point from point centroid c1 is shorter compared to the distance of the same data point from centroid C2. This means that this data point will be assigned to the cluster C1.

Let us take another data point, (15,12):

Euclidean Distance from the Cluster Centroid C1 = (5,3) IS 13.45

Euclidean Distance from the Cluster Centroid C2 = (10,15) IS 5.83

The distance from the data point to the centroid C2 is shorter, hence it will be assigned to the cluster C2.

Now that the data points have been assigned to the right clusters, the next step should involve calculation of the new centroid values. The values should be calculated by determining the means of the coordinates for the data points belonging to a certain cluster.

If for example for C1 we had allocated the following two data points to the cluster:

(5, 3) and (24, 10). The new value for x coordinate will be the mean of the two:

x = (5 + 24) / 2

x = 14.5

The new value for y will be:

y = (3 + 10) / 2

y = 13/2

y = 6.5

The new centroid value for the c1 will be (14.5, 6.5).

This should be done for c2 and the entire process be repeated. The iterations should be repeated until when the centroid values do not update any more. This means if for example, you do three iterations, you may find that the updated values for centroids c1 and c2 in the fourth iterations are equal to what we had in iteration 3. This means that your data cannot be clustered any further.

You are now familiar with how the K-Means algorithm works. Let us discuss how you can implement it in the Scikit-Learn library.

Let us first import all the libraries that we need to use:

import matplotlib.pyplot as plt

import numpy as np

from sklearn.cluster import KMeans

Data Preparation

We should now prepare the data that is to be used. We will be creating a **numpy array** with a total of 10 rows and 2 columns. So, why have we chosen to work with a numpy array? It is because Scikit-Learn library can work with the numpy array data inputs without the need for preprocessing. Let us create it:

X = np.array([[5,3], [10,15], [15,12], [24,10], [30,45], [85,70], [71,80], [60,78], [55,52], [80,91],])

Visualizing the Data

Now that we have the data, we can create a plot and see how the data points are distributed. We will then be able to tell whether there are any clusters at the moment:

plt.scatter(X[:,0],X[:,1], label='True Position')

```
plt.show()
```

The code gives the following plot:

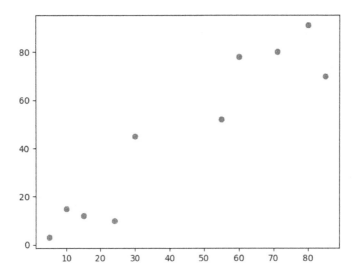

If we use our eyes, we will probably make two clusters from the above data, one at the bottom with five points and another one at the top with five points. We now need to investigate whether this is what the K-Means clustering algorithm will do.

Creating Clusters

We have seen that we can form two clusters from the data points, hence the value of K is now 2. These two clusters can be created by running the following code:

```
kmeans_clusters = KMeans(n_clusters=2)
```

```
kmeans_clusters.fit(X)
```

We have created an object named *kmeans_clusters* and 2 have been used as the value for the parameter *n_clusters*. We have then called the *fit()* method on this object and passed the data we have in our numpy array as the parameter to the method.

We can now have a look at the centroid values that the algorithm has created for the final clusters:

print (kmeans_clusters.cluster_centers_)

This returns the following:

```
[[ 16.8    17. ]
 [ 70.2    74.2]]
```

The first row above gives us the coordinates for the first centroid, which is, (16.8, 17). The second row gives us the coordinates of the second centroid, which is, (70.2, 74.2). If you followed the manual process of calculating the values of these, they should be the same. This will be an indication that the K-Means algorithm worked well.

The following script will help us see the data point labels:

print(kmeans_clusters.labels_)

This returns the following:

```
[0 0 0 0 0 1 1 1 1 1]
```

The above output shows a one-dimensional array of 10 elements which correspond to the clusters that are assigned to the 10 data points. You clearly see that we first have a sequence of zeroes which shows that the first 5 points have been clusterd together while the last five points have been clustered together. Note that the 0 and 1 have no mathematical significance but they have simply been used to represent the cluster IDs. If we had three clusters, then the last one would have been represented using 2's.

We can now plot the data points and see how they have been clustered. We need to plot the data points alongside their assigned labels to be able to distinguish the clusters. Just execute the script given below:

plt.scatter(X[:,0],X[:,1],
c=kmeans_clusters.labels_, cmap='rainbow')

```
        plt.show()
```

The script returns the following plot:

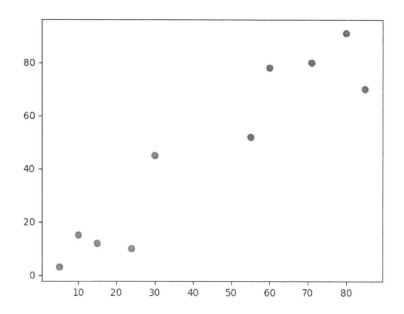

We have simply plotted the first column of the array named X against the second column. At the same time, we have passed *kmeans_labels_* as the value for parameter c which corresponds to the labels.

Note the use of the parameter *cmap='rainbow'*. This parameter helps us to choose the color type for the different data points.

As you expected, the first five points have been clustered together at the bottom left and assigned a similar color. The remaining five points have been clustered together at the top right and assigned one unique color.

We can choose to plot the points together with the centroid coordinates for every cluster to see how the positioning of the centroid affects clustering. Let us use three clusters to see how they affect the centroids. The following script will help you to create the plot:

plt.scatter(X[:,0],   X[:,1],
c=kmeans_clusters.labels_, cmap='rainbow')

plt.scatter(kmeans_clusters.cluster_centers_[:,0]
,kmeans_clusters.cluster_centers_[:,1],
color='black')

    plt.show()

The script returns the following plot:

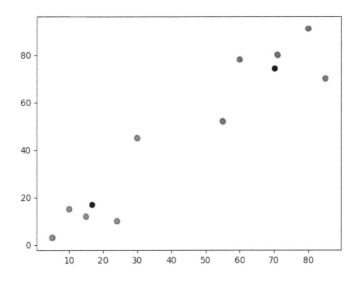

We have chosen to plot the centroid points in black color.

Chapter 7 Support Vector Machines

SVMs fall under the category of supervised machine learning algorithms and are highly applied classification and regression problems. It is known for its ability to handle nonlinear input spaces. It is highly applied in applications like intrusion detection, face detection, classification of news articles, emails and web pages, handwriting recognition and classification of genes.

The algorithm works by segregating the data points in the best way possible. The distance between the nearest points is referred to as the *margin*. The goal is to choose a hyperplane with the maximum possible margin between the support vectors in a given dataset.

To best understand how this algorithm works, let us first implement it in Scikit-Learn library. Our goal is to predict whether a bank currency note is fake or authentic. We will use the attributes of the note including variance of the image, the skewness of the wavelet transformed image, curtosis of the image and entropy of the image. Since this is a binary classification algorithm, let us use the SVM classification algorithm.

If we have a linearly separable data with two dimensions, the goal of a typical machine learning algorithm is to identify a boundary that will divide the data so as to minimize the misclassification error. In most cases, one gets several lines with all these lines correctly classifying the data.

SVM is different from the other classification algorithms in the way it selects the decision boundary maximizing the distance from the nearest data points for all classes. The goal of SVM is not to find the decision boundary only, but to find the most optimal decision boundary.

The most optimal decision boundary refers to the decision boundary with the maximum margin from nearest points of all classes. The nearest points from the decision boundary maximizing the distance between the decision boundary and the points are known as *support vectors*. For the case of support vector machines, the decision boundary is known as *maximum margin classifier* **or** *maximum margin hyper plane.*

A complex mathematics is involved in the calculation of the support vectors; determine the margin between the decision boundary and support vectors and maximizing the margin.

Let us begin by importing the necessary libraries:

import numpy as np

import pandas as pd

import matplotlib.pyplot as plt

This dataset can be downloaded from the following URL:

https://drive.google.com/file/d/13nw-uRXPY8XIZQxKRNZ3yYlho-CYm_Qt/view

Download and store it on your local machine. I have saved the file in the same directory as my Python scripts and given it the name *bank_note.csv*.

Importing the Dataset

We will use the *read_csv* method provided by the Pandas library to read the data and import it into our workspace. This can be done as follows:

dataset = pd.read_csv("bank_note.csv")

Let us call the shape method to print the shape of the data for us:

```
print(dataset.shape)
```

This returns the following:

(1372, 5)

This shows that there are 1372 columns and 5 columns in the dataset. Let us print the first 5 rows of the dataset:

```
print(dataset.head())
```

Again, this may return an error because of lack of the output information. Let us solve this using the Python's sys library. You should now have the following code:

import numpy as np

import pandas as pd

import matplotlib.pyplot as plt

import sys

```
sys.__stdout__=sys.stdout
```
dataset = pd.read_csv("bank_note.csv")

```
print(dataset.head())
```

The code returns the following output:

```
   Variance  Skewness  Curtosis  Entropy  Class
0   3.62160    8.6661   -2.8073 -0.44699      0
1   4.54590    8.1674   -2.4586 -1.46210      0
2   3.86600   -2.6383    1.9242  0.10645      0
3   3.45660    9.5228   -4.0112 -3.59440      0
4   0.32924   -4.4552    4.5718 -0.98880      0
```

All attributes of the data are numeric as shown above. Even the last attribute is numeric as its values are either 0 or 1.

Preprocessing the Data

It is now time to subdivide the above data into attributes and labels as well as training and test sets. The following code will help us subdivide the data into attributes and labels:

X = dataset.drop('Class', axis=1)

y = dataset['Class']

The first line above helps us store all the columns of the dataset into variable **X**, except the *class* column. The *drop()* function has helped us exclude the *Class* column from this. The second line has then helped us store the *Class* column into variable *y*. The variable **X** now has attributes while the variable *y* now has the corresponding labels.

We have achieved the goal of diving the dataset into attributes and labels. The next step is to divide the dataset into training and test sets. Scikit-learn has a library known as *model_selection* which provides us with a method named *train_test_split* that we can use to divide the data into training and test sets.

First, let us import the *train_test_split* method:

from sklearn.model_selection import train_test_split

The following script will then help us to perform the split:

X_train, X_test, y_train, y_test = train_test_split(X, y, test_size = 0.20)

Training the Algorithm

Now that the data has been split into training and test sets, we should now train the SVM on the training set. Scikit-Learn comes with a library known as *svm* which has built-in classes for various SVM algorithms.

In this case, we will be doing a classification task, hence we will use the support vector classifier class (SVC). The takes a single parameter, that is, the kernel type. For a simple SVM, the parameter should be set to **"linear"** since the simple SVMs can only classify data that is linearly separable.

We will call the *fit* method of SVC to train the algorithm on our training set. The training set should be passed as a parameter to the *fit* method. Let us first import the SVC class from Scikit-Learn:

from sklearn.svm import SVC

Now run the following code:

svc_classifier = SVC(kernel='linear')

svc_classifier.fit(X_train, y_train)

Making Predicting

We should use the SVC class for making predictions. Note that the predictions will be made on the test data. Here is the code for making predictions:

pred_y = svc_classifier.predict(X_test)

Evaluating the Accuracy of the Algorithm

In classification tasks, we use confusion matrix, recall, precision and F1 as the metrics. Scikit-Learn has the *metrics* library which provides us with the *confusion_matrix* and *classification_report* methods which can help us find the values of these metrics. The following code can help us find the value for these metrics:

First, let us import the above methods from the Scikit-Learn library:

from sklearn.metrics import confusion_matrix, classification_report

Here is the code that can help in doing the evaluation:

print(confusion_matrix(y_test,pred_y))

print(classification_report(y_test,pred_y))

The code returns the following:

```
[[160    1]
 [   1 113]]
              precision    recall  f1-score   support

           0      0.99      0.99      0.99       161
           1      0.99      0.99      0.99       114

avg / total       0.99      0.99      0.99       275
```

The output given above shows that the algorithm did a good task. An average of 99% for the above metrics is not bad.

Let us give another example of how to implement SVM in Scikit-Learn using the Iris dataset. We had already loaded the Iris dataset, a dataset that shows details of flowers in terms of sepal and petal measurements, that is, width and length. We can now learn from the data, and then make a prediction for unknown data. These calls for us to create an estimator then call its fit method.

This is demonstrated in the script given below:

from sklearn import svm

from sklearn import datasets

Loading the dataset

iris = datasets.load_iris()

clf = svm.LinearSVC()

learn from the dataset

clf.fit(iris.data, iris.target)

predict unseen data

clf.predict([[6.2, 4.2, 3.5, 0.35]])

Changing model parameters using the attributes ending with an underscore

print(clf.coef_)

The code will return the following output:

```
[[ 0.18423824  0.45123312 -0.80793878 -0.45071592]
 [ 0.05187834 -0.88969839  0.40345845 -0.93664852]
 [-0.85062306 -0.98667154  1.38105171  1.86536558]]
```

We now have the predicted values for our data. Note that we imported both *datasets* and *svm* from the scikit-learn library. After loading the dataset, a model was fitted/created by learning patterns from the data. This was done by calling the *fit()* method. Note that the *LinearSVC()*method helps us to create an estimator for the support vector classifier, on which we are to create the model. We have then passed in new data for which we need to make a prediction.

Chapter 8 Variables and Data Types

A software application consists of two fundamental parts: Logic and Data. Logic consists of the functionalities that are applied on data to accomplish a particular task. Application data can be stored in memory or hard disk. Files and databases are used to store data on hard disk. In memory, data is stored in the form of variables.

Definition of Variable

Variable in programming is a memory location used to store some value. Whenever you store a value in a variable, that value is actually being stored at physical location in memory. Variables can be thought of as reference to physical memory location. The size of the memory reserved for a variable depends upon the type of value stored in the variable.

Creating a Variable

It is very easy to create a variable in Python. The assignment operator "=" is used for this purpose. The value to the left of the assignment operator is the variable identifier or name of the variable. The value to the right of the operator is the value assigned to the variable. Take a look at the following code snippet.

```
Name  = 'Mike'        # A string variable

Age   = 15            # An integer variable

Score = 102.5         # A floating type variable

Pass  = True          # A boolean Variable
```

In the script above we created four different types of variables. You can see that we did not specify the type of variable with the variable name. For instance we did not write "string Name" or "int Age". We only wrote the variable name. This is because Python is a loosely typed language. Depending upon the value being stored in a variable, Python assigns type to the variable at runtime. For instance when Python interpreter interprets the line "Age = 15", it checks the type of the value which is integer in this case. Hence, Python understands that Age is an integer type variable.

To check type of a variable, pass the variable name to "type" function as shown below:

```
type(Age)
```

You will see that the above script, when run, prints "int" in the output which is basically the type of Age variable.

Python allows multiple assignment which means that you can assign one value to multiple variables at the same time. Take a look at the following script:

Age = Number = Point = 20 #Multiple Assignment

print (Age)

print (Number)

print (Point)

In the script above, integer 20 is assigned to three variables: Age, Number and Point. If you print the value of these three variables, you will see 20 thrice in the output.

Python Data Types

A programming application needs to store variety of data. Consider scenario of a banking application that needs to store customer information. For instance, a person's name and mobile number; whether he is a defaulter or not; collection of items that he/she has loaned and so on. To store such variety of information, different data types are required. While you can create custom data types in the form of classes, Python provides six standard data types out of the box. They are:

- Strings
- Numbers
- Booleans

- Lists
- Tuples
- Dictionaries

Strings

Python treats string as sequence of characters. To create strings in Python, you can use single as well as double quotes. Take a look at the following script:

first_name = 'mike' # String with single quotation

last_name = " johns" # String with double quotation

full_name = first_name + last_name # string concatenation using +

print(full_name)

In the above script we created three string variables: first_name, last_name and full_name. String with single quotes is used to initialize the variable "first_name" while string with double quotes initializes the variable "last_name". The variable full_name contains the concatenation of the first_name and last_name variables. Running the above script returns following output:

mike johns

Numbers

There are four types of numeric data in python:

- int (Stores integer e.g 10)
- float (Stores floating point numbers e.g 2.5)
- long (Stores long integer such as 48646684333)
- complex (Complex number such as 7j+4847k)

To create a numeric Python variable, simply assign a number to variable. In the following script we create four different types of numeric objects and print them on the console.

```
int_num = 10      # integer

float_num = 156.2  #float

long_num = -0.5977485613454646  #long

complex_num = -.785+7J #Complex


print(int_num)

print(float_num)

print(long_num)

print(complex_num)
```

The output of the above script will be as follows:

```
10
156.2
-0.5977485613454646
(-0.785+7j)
```

Boolean

Boolean variables are used to store Boolean values. True and False are the two Boolean values in Python. Take a look at the following example:

defaulter = True

has_car = False

print(defaulter and has_car)

In the script above we created two Boolean variables "defaulter" and "has_car" with values True and False respectively. We then print the result of the AND operation on both of these variables. Since the AND operation between True and False returns false, you will see false in the output. We will study more about the logical operators in the next chapter.

Lists

In Python, List data type is used to store collection of values. Lists are similar to arrays in any other programming language. However Python lists can store values of different types. To create a list opening and closing square brackets are used. Each item in the list is separated from the other with a comma. Take a look at the following example.

cars = ['Honda', 'Toyota', 'Audi', 'Ford', 'Suzuki', 'Mercedez']

print(len(cars))   #finds total items in string

print(cars)

In the script above we created a list named cars. The list contains six string values i.e. car names. Next we printed the size of the list using len function. Finally we print the list on console.

The output looks like this:

```
6
['Honda', 'Toyota', 'Audi', 'Ford', 'Suzuki', 'Mercedez']
```

Tuples

Tuples are similar to lists with two major differences. Firstly, opening and closing braces are used to create tuples instead of lists that use square brackets. Secondly, tuple once created is immutable which means that you cannot change tuple values once it is created. The following example clarifies this concept.

```
cars = ['Honda', 'Toyota', 'Audi', 'Ford', 'Suzuki',
'Mercedez']


cars2 = ('Honda', 'Toyota', 'Audi', 'Ford', 'Suzuki',
'Mercedez')


cars [3] = 'WV'


cars2 [3] = 'WV'
```

In the above script we created a list named cars and a tuple named cars2. Both the list and tuple contains list of car names. We then try to update the third index of the list as well as tuple with a new value. The list will be updated but an error will be thrown while trying to update the tuple's third index. This is due to the fact that tuple, once created cannot be modified with new values. The error looks like this:

Dictionaries

Dictionaries store collection of data in the form of key-value pairs. Each key-value pair is separated from the other via comma. Keys and values are separated from each other via colon. Dictionary items can be accessed via index as well as keys. To create dictionaries you need to add key-value pairs inside opening and closing parenthesis. Take a look at the following example.

cars = {'Name':'Audi', 'Model': 2008, 'Color':'Black'}

print(cars['Color'])

print(cars.keys())

print(cars.values())

In the above script we created a dictionary named cars. The dictionary contains three key-value pairs i.e. 3 items. To access value, we can pass key to the brackets that follow dictionary name. Similarly we can use keys() and values() methods to retrieve all the keys and values from a dictionary, respectively. The output of the script above looks like this:

```
Black
dict_keys(['Name', 'Model', 'Color'])
dict_values(['Audi', 2008, 'Black'])
```

Chapter 9 How to install the Python Interpreter, how to use the Python Shell, IDLE and write your first program ✑

Python installation is dependent upon the OS on your computer as well as the source of the Python installation you are using. Python can be obtained from a number of different sources, some of which are modified versions of the official releases.

The following discussion will look at the installation procedure for the 3 major supported operating systems from the official source at python.org. Installation for other operating systems should be similar to one of these three. Please see python.org for installers and instructions for those systems.

The installers on pythons.org contain the python interpreter, the IDLE integrated development environment and the python shell.

Following is an OS specific description to installing and accessing each.

Mac OS X:

Mac OS X comes with Python 2 preinstalled. The exact version of python will depend on the version of OS X currently running on your system and can be determined by opening the terminal app and entering the following at the prompt:

python –V

which should return a result similar to:

Python 2.6.1

Python 3 can also be installed on OS X with no need to uninstall 2.x. To check for a 3.x installation open the terminal app and enter the following at the prompt:

Python3 –V

which should return a result similar to:

Python 3.6.4

By default, OS X will not have python 3.x installed. If you wish to use python 3.x, it can be installed with binary installers for OS X available at python.org.

Those installers will install the interpreter, the IDLE development tools and the python shell for python 3.x. Unlike python 2.x, those tools are installed as standard applications in the applications folder.

Running IDLE and the python shell in OS X is dependent on the version of Python you are using and your personal preference. The IDLE/shell applications in Python 2.x and 3.x can be started from the terminal window by entering the following commands:

For python 2.x:

Idle

For Python 3.x:

idle3

As mentioned above, Python 3 also installs IDLE as a standard application in the Python folder within the Applications older. To start the IDLE/Shell program from the desktop simply open that folder and double click the IDLE application.

Python can also be accessed as a command line terminal application within OS X. With a terminal window open, simply enter the following:

Python 2.x:

Python

and you will get a response like:

Python 2.6.1 (r261:67515, Jun 24 2010, 21:47:49) [GCC 4.2.1 (Apple Inc. build 5646)] on darwin Type "help", "copyright", "credits" or "license" for more information.

>>>

Python 3.x:

python3

and you will get a response like:

Python 3.6.4 (v3.6.4:d48ecebad5, Dec 18 2017, 21:07:28)
 [GCC 4.2.1 (Apple Inc. build 5666) (dot 3)] on darwin
 Type "help", "copyright", "credits" or "license" for more information.

>>>

The >>> prompt allows direct entry of python commands which will be detailed in greater depth later.

Windows:

Once setup correctly, python can used from the command line with either command.exe or the windows power shell.

Alternatively, the standard installation adds Python IDLE to the start menu. Selecting that will bring up the IDLE application to allow you to start creating your first script.

Linux

If you are using one of the many flavors of Linux you can check for the presence of python by typing

python -V

at a shell command prompt. If python is installed, the installed version should be returned like

Python 3.6.4

If not, an error should be returned.

Installing and/or updating can vary depending on the Linux distribution you are using. Please consult the documentation for your linux distribution for more information.

Python Interpreter, IDLE, and the Shell

A standard installation of Python from python.org, contains documentation, licensing information and 3 main executable files which are used to develop and run python scripts.

Let's take a brief look at each of these three programs and the role each plays in python programming.

Python Interpreter

The python interpreter is the program responsible for executing the scripts you write. The interpreter converts the .py script files into bytecode instructions and then processes them according to the code written in the file.

Python IDLE

IDLE is the Python integrated development and learning environment. It contains all of the tools you will need to develop programs in Python including the shell, a text editor and debugging tools.

Depending on your python version and operating system, IDLE can be very basic or have an extensive array of options that can be setup.

For example, on Mac OS X, the text editor can be setup with several code indentation and highlighting options which can make your programs much easier to read and work with.

If the text editor in IDLE does not offer the sophistication you need, there are several aftermarket text editors which support Python script highlighting, autocomplete and other features that make script writing easier.

Python Shell

The shell is an interactive, command line driven interface to the python interpreter.

In the python shell, commands are entered at the >>> prompt. Anything that is entered at the prompt must be in proper python syntax, incorrect entries will return a syntax error like

SyntaxError: invalid syntax

When a command is entered, it is specific to that shell and has the lifetime of the shell.

For example, if you assign a variable a value such as:

```
>>>X=10
```

Then the variable is assigned an integer value of 10.

That value will be maintained until the shell is closed, restarted or the value is changed.

If another shell window is opened, the value of X will not be accessible in the new window.

When a command is entered and accepted, the code is executed. If the entered code generates a response, the response will be output to the specified device. If it does not, such as simply assigning a variable as above, then another prompt (>>>) is shown and additional commands can be entered.

This can be useful for a number of simple tasks, testing simple functions and getting a feel for how commands work.

As an example, enter the following:

```
>>>X=10
 >>>Y=5
 >>>print(X)
 10
 >>>print(Y)
 5
 >>>print(X+Y)
 15
```

This demonstrates a couple of things.
First, we assign the two variables X and Y values.

Both variables retain their values within the shell. It also shows that the way we defined the variables was acceptable. If it is acceptable in the shell, it will be acceptable in a script.

If a command is not acceptable, it will return an error or exception.

For example if we ask for the length of X with the following command

>>>print(len(X))

Then the following is returned:

Traceback (most recent call last):
  File "<pyshell#12>", line 1, in <module>
    print(len(X))
 TypeError: object of type 'int' has no len()

The error returned usually will provide some valuable information as to why the error occurred.

In this case, it is telling us that we assigned an integer value to X.

The len() command gives the length of a string so we are getting this error because the type of data held by the variable does not match the requirements of the function called.

If instead we had used

```
>>>print(len(str(X)))
2
```

In this case, we are using the str() command to convert the value of X into a string.

We are then using len() to get the length of that string, which is 2 characters.

This can be loosely translated into

$$X=12 \rightarrow str(X)='12' \rightarrow len('12')=2$$

We can continue to use the shell to explore other things like different ways to assign variable values.

For example, rather than explicitly assigning values on a per line basis, variables can be assigned as comma separated groups.

```
>>>X,Y = 20,12
 >>>print(X,Y)
 20 12
```

Script Editor

To create our first program, open the text editor.

To open it in a GUI OS like OS X or Windows, select File->New from the IDLE menus.

In non-GUI implementations .py files can be created in a terminal text editor like VI or VIM. Please see documentation on those programs for information on working in them.

Once a text window is open we can simply enter our program code.

In this case, we will write a quick program for calculating the volume of a cylinder. The formula is $V=(\pi r^2)*h$ where r is the radius and h is the height.

While this program will be extremely simple, and could easily be done just using the shell, it will show several fundamentally important things in Python programming.

The first step will be to import the math library.

Many functions available in python are stored in libraries. These libraries typically house functions which are grouped by task such as math.

If the proper library is not loaded when prior to making a call to that library, an error such as

```
Traceback      (most      recent      call      last):
    File  "<pyshell#22>",  line  1,  in  <module>
                            print(math.exp(2))
  NameError: name 'math' is not defined
```

will be displayed. This error is telling you that math is not defined.

Since math is part of a Python standard library this tells you that the library was not imported prior to execution of the request for the math keyword.

In the text editor, enter the lines as follows

```
# import math library
 import math
```

The #is the python comment symbol. Anything between that and the end of the line is ignored by the interpreter.

One of the key advantages of Python scripting is readability so it is very important (as it is in all programing) to be diligent about commenting.

Comments will make it easier to debug your code later and will make it easier for someone else to look at your work and see how the program works.

In many cases, it also forces you to slow down and think out the programming process as you go which will lead to cleaner and better organized code.

Next, we need to set up our variables.

This can be done anywhere within a script as long as they are defined prior to calling for their value.

If a variable is called before it is defined, a 'name not defined' exception will be displayed and program execution will halt.

```
# assign variables

r=5 # radius
 h=10 # height
 V-0 # volume
```

While V does not need to be explicitly defined, here it is considered good practice to do so because it makes the code is easier to understand.

Next, we do the actual volume calculation.

```
# calculate volume of a cylinder
 V=(math.pi*math.pow(r,2))*h #
volume=(π*r^2)*h
```

Next, to see the result we use the print function, which will output the result to the console.

```
# output the result
 print(V)
```

The complete program looks like this

```
# import math

import math

# assign variables
 r=5 # radius
 h=10 # height
 V=0 # volume

# calculate volume of a cylinder
 V=(math.pi*math.pow(r,2))*h #
volume=(π*r^2)*h

# output the result
 print(V)
```

You can save the program to your hard drive, let's call it cylinder.py.

Python views files ending in .py as script files so it is important to always save your scripts with the .py extension. Once we have a saved script file, we can go ahead and run it.

Chapter 10 Strings

Earlier in the variables section we learned a little about strings. Strings and string functions are one of the strengths of the Python language.

It has many built in string handling and manipulation features and many more are available through external libraries. Previously, we discussed accessing substrings using the [:] nomenclature, as well as concatenating strings using the '+' operator.

Python offers inline string formatting similar to that in C/C++ through the use of the % special character. % followed by any one of a number of formatting characters allows variable information to be inserted into formatted strings for display or storage.

Those special characters include:

%c – character
%d – signed decimal
%e – lower case e exponent
%E – upper case E exponent
%f – floating point number
%g – the smaller of %e/%f
%G – the smaller of %E/%F
%i – signed integer
%s – string
%u – unsigned integer

%o – octal

%x – lower case hexadecimal

%X – upper case hexadecimal

These can be used as follows to format text on the fly:

>>> print('%s scored %i in game one of the playoffs' % ('John', 32))

John scored 32 in game one of the playoffs

As shown the values for %s and %i are dynamically inserted into the output text based on the input values provided in parenthesis.

While in this example, the values are given explicitly, they can also be provided as variables. Care must be taken to insure the variable types and the formatting characters match. In other words, do not specify %i and provide a string variable as the source.

These formatting characters also have a number of modifiers that alter or specify their output.

These include:

*   specifies width or precision

-       justify left

+   show sign

<sp>   left padding with spaces

show leading 0's in octal output or leading 0x in hexidecimal

0   left padding with 0's

    %%   literal % (allows printing a % symbol in the string)

    (var)   key value for dictionary elements

    m.n.   for floating point numbers this is the minimum width and number of decimal places

```
>>> print('%s spent $%3.2f at the store last night' % ('John', 12.8975))
```

John spent $12.90 at the store last night

%3.2f formats the floating point number to 2 decimal places.

The % nomenclature is considered the 'old way' of handling string formatting. The new format is to enclose the formatted text in braces while calling the format function like this:

```
>>> print('{} spent ${:2.2f} at the store last night'.format('John', 12.8975))
```

John spent $12.90 at the store last night

In this case, the first insert is a set of empty braces. This is what is classified as an autofill, or more specifically that it is filled by the items in the format command in the order it's called.

The second set of braces then autofills with the second item in the format statement. In that second statement we used a ':' to specify that a formatting modifier is included.

Alternatively, we can manually select which items within the format command get inserted into the string as follows:

>>> print('Item 3={2}, Item 2={1}, Item 4={3}, Item 1={0}'.format('1','2','3','4'))

Item 3=3, Item 2=2, Item 4=4, Item 1=1

A dictionaries key value pair can also be used to fill in strings dynamically as well. For example:

>>> 'My Name is {firstname} and I am {age} years old'.format(firstname='John', age=29)

'My Name is John and I am 29 years old'

        Or..

>>>   testd={'firstname':   'John',   'age':   29}
 >>> 'My Name is {firstname} and I am {age} years old'.format(**testd)

'My Name is John and I am 29 years old'

The ** operator is the exponent operator when applied to numerical variables. When applied as shown to a dictionary, it force splits the dictionary into its component entities.

If testd={'firstname': 'John', 'age': 29} then **testd=(firstname='John', age=29) so the use of the operator functionally converts the contents of the dictionary variable in the second example into the format of the first example.

Python has a large number of built in string methods. These do a wide range of everyday string manipulation functions in a single command that would require more elaborate programming in other languages.

As of this writing there are 44 different methods available and as the language evolves more are added. Due that evolution, the not all of the 44 will be available on all versions of Python.

Because of that fact, and the sheer volume of methods, covering all of them and their use is beyond the scope of this book.

Here are a few of the more commonly used examples and how to use them. Reference to all of them is available from the docs on python.org.

> *str.lower()* - converts a string to all lower case

```
>>> str.lower('Hello')
 'hello'
```

str.upper() - converts a string to all upper case

```
>>> str.upper('Hello')
 'HELLO'
```

These functions convert text to all lower or upper case respectively. This is a common operation when checking for non-case sensitive equality in string values.

```
>>> print('Hello'=='hello')
 False
```

```
>>> print(str.lower('Hello')=='hello')
 True
```

str.strip([char]) – strips characters from the beginning and end of a string. It removes only the characters specified by char. If char is not specified, it strips whitespace. This is a commonly used command to remove leading and trailing spaces from user input.

```
>>> print(str.strip('    Hello      '))
 Hello
```

```
>>> print(str.strip('    #--Comments--#      ', ' ' #-
 '))
 Comments
```

str.split([,delimiter]) – splits a string into individual list entries using delimiter as the split point.

```
>>> str.split('A,b,CC,ASD,The end', ',')
 ['A', 'b', 'CC', 'ASD', 'The end']
```

```
>>> str.split('www.mywebsite.com', '.')
 ['www', 'mywebsite', 'com']
```

```
>>> myweb='WWW.WEBSITE.COM'
 >>> myweb.split('.')
 ['www', 'website', 'com']
```

Chapter 11 Control Flow
Introduction

Went to sleep you starts execution of the program code, it starts from the main function and terminates at the end of the code, which is usually the end of main function. The statements that are executed in sequence are nothing but the part of the program. Most of the programs, which we have learned until now are simple straight line programs. These programs have a steady and sequential flow.

To break the flow of control, we have control flow statements in C++. Please control flow statements help the programmer to change the path of the CPU. Some of the control flow statements discussed below.

Halt: this is the most widely used and the basic control statement in C++. You can perform a halt with the exit function. The exit functional is defined in the header cstdlib. Here is a small example showing the use of exit function.

```
1  #include <cstdlib> // needed for exit()
2  #include <iostream>
3  int main()
4  {
5      std::cout << 1;
6      exit(0); // terminate and return 0 to operating system
7      // The following statements never execute
8      std::cout << 2;
9      return 0;
10 }
```

In the above sample code the flow of control is broken and it will never reach the statements that are written below the exit statement. These types of statements give the programmer the authority to stop the program when required.

Jumps: Jump is also a basic controls statement in C++. Using this statement will make the CPU to jump to a different statement. Continue, break and goto are used to perform different types of jumping operations.

Conditional branches: these are flow control statements which change the part of the flow of control depending on the value of a given expression. The 'if' statement is the most basic type of the conditional branch statements. Example:

```
int main()
{
    // do A
    if (expression)
        // do B
    else
        // do C
    // do D
}
```

In the sample code given above, there are two possible paths the flow of control can take. If it is it true the CPU will go and execute A, B and D. But if the condition turns out to be false the flow of control will go and execute A, C and D statements.

Conditionals

Conditionals allow you to form a junction in the code and send it off on various paths, rather than keeping it as a linear code. C++ conditionals are if statements - if something is false, the program should execute one piece of code, another if it is true:

```
1  int a = 1;
2  {
3  if(a < 2)
4  {
5      cout << "a is less than 2!\n";
6  }
```

You know what lines 1 and 5 mean but line 3 is a little different – this is an if statement. What it is doing is checking to see if the integer variable is less than 2. If it is, it will run one piece of code, if not, it will carry on as normal. If you compile and run what is written here, you will see printed on your screen "a is less than 2!".

Loops

Loops are used in the programs where the code is to be used repeatedly. They will put the code into a loop till the condition is satisfied. Imagine if you have to write a code, which prints numbers from 1 to 100 in a new line each. Writing the code for such programs will be very difficult and time taking. For such situations we use loops. Loops keep the flow of control in the loop till the condition is satisfied.

So our code now reads user inputs, it can do a variety of different things based on those inputs but now we are going to look at making that code do the same things over and over again but with slightly different parameters. To do this, we need to use a loop, which is a piece of code that is repeated a number of different times until it's achieved what it needed to do and a specific C++ condition has been met. C++ has three different types of loop:

- while
- for
- do

The WHILE loop is the easiest and looks very similar to an if statement:

```
1  int userInput = 0;
2
3  while(userInput != 10)
4  {
5      cin >> userInput;
6  }
```

What the WHILE loop is doing here is saying that while whatever the user input variable is not equal to 10, the code needs to get some input from the user. In C++, the exclamation mark (!) means not, so ! = means not equal.

In this case, if the user input had already been 10 then the code would not have been executed and the loop will be ignored. In all truthfulness, the WHILE loop is just seen as an extended IF statement that goes back inside of itself after the code is run.

Before we move on, I want to show what an INFINITE loop looks like, a loop that just keeps on going:

```
1   while(1 == 1)
2   {
3   cout << "a";
4   }
```

As you can see, it is saying that if 1 is equal to 1, print an a, and so on.

The next easiest loop is the DO WHILE loop, as it is similar to the while loop.

```
1   int userInput = 0;
2
3   do
4   {
5       cin >> userInput;
6   } while (userInput != 10);
```

While it looks somewhat different to the WHILE loop, it is doing essentially the same job with one important difference – the WHILE loop checks a conditional and looks to see if it is true but the DO WHILE loop runs code and then checks if the conditional is true or not. Because of this, all of the code is guaranteed to run.

The third type of C++ loop is FOR and this one is the most complicated one. Once you understand it though, you will find that it is the most powerful. Here, we are just going to look at simple usage:

```
1   int i = 0;
2   {
3     for(i = 2; i < 10; ++i)
4     {
5         cout << i << "\n";
6     }
```

What this code is saying is, start off by setting the value of i to 2. Then it goes on to say that, as long as i is less than 10 it should output the value onto the screen and then increment i. You must bear one thing in mind – all of the variables that are used in the first line of a FOR loop have to be the same variable. It is also important to remember that, unlike a WHILE loop, the first statement is an assignment and not a conditional.

This sort of loop is useful if you want to get through a number of pieces of data and I'll talk more about that in the next section. For now, as you can see, the most useful thing it can do is chuck out a sequence of numbers. That is a useful talks and it brings us neatly on to the next section.

If statement:

The 'if' statement is the most basic condition right statement in C++. It will check for a given condition and will change the flow of control depending on the outcome of the condition.

Here is a simple code which has an 'if' statement and It.

291

```
1    #include <iostream>
2    int main()
3    {
4        std::cout << "Enter a number: ";
5        int x;
6        std::cin >> x;
7        if (x > 10)
8            std::cout << x << "is greater than 10\n";
9        else
10            std::cout << x << "is not greater than 10\n";
11        return 0;
12    }
```

We already know that if statement takes a statement as the condition. We also know that we can use a block in place of a single statement. This means we can use a Block inside an if statement as a condition. The following example shows a Block being used in an if statement as a condition.

```
1    #include <iostream>
2    int main()
3    {
4        std::cout << "Enter a number: ";
5        int x;
6        std::cin >> x;
7        if (x > 10)
8            {
9            // both statements will be executed if x > 10
10            std::cout << "You entered " << x << "\n";
11            std::cout << x << "is greater than 10\n";
12            }
13        else
14            {
15            // both statements will be executed if x <= 10
16            std::cout << "You entered " << x << "\n";
17            std::cout << x << "is not greater than 10\n";
18            }
19        return 0;
20    }
```

You can also place one if statement inside another if statement. An if statement which has another if statement in it is called a nested if.

Here are two examples, which will help you to understand the nested if better.

Example 1:

```
1  #include <iostream>
2  using namespace std;
3
4  int main ()
5  {
6      // local variable declaration:
7      int a = 100;
8      int b = 200;
9
10     // check the boolean condition
11     if( a == 100 )
12     {
13         // if condition is true then check the following
14         if( b == 200 )
15         {
16             // if condition is true then print the following
17             cout << "Value of a is 100 and b is 200" << endl;
18         }
19     }
20     cout << "Exact value of a is : " << a << endl;
21     cout << "Exact value of b is : " << b << endl;
22
23     return 0;
24  }
```

Example 2:

```
1   #include <iostream>
2   int main()
3   {
4       std::cout << "Enter a number: ";
5       int x;
6       std::cin >> x;
7       if (x > 10) // outer if statement
8           // it is bad coding style to nest if statements this way
9           if (x < 20) // inner if statement
10              std::cout << x << "is between 10 and 20\n";
11          // who does this else belong to?
12          else
13              std::cout << x << "is greater than 20\n";
14      return 0;
15  }
```

You can encase an if statement into a block and you can attach an else statement to it. You can see how with the below example.

```
1   #include <iostream>
2   int main()
3   {
4       std::cout << "Enter a number: ";
5       int x;
6       std::cin >> x;
7       if (x > 10)
8       {
9           if (x < 20)
10              std::cout << x << "is between 10 and 20";
11      }
12      else // attached to outer if statement
13          std::cout << x << "is less than 10\n";
14      ;
15  }
```

If statements with logical operators

You can use if statements with logical operators for checking multiple conditions at the same time. The sample code is given below.

Example:

```
1   #include <iostream>
2   int main()
3   {
4       std::cout << "Enter an integer: ";
5       int x;
6       std::cin >> x;
7       std::cout << "Enter another integer: ";
8       int y;
9       std::cin >> y;
10      if (x > 0 && y > 0) // && is logical and -- checks if both conditions are true
11          std::cout << "Both numbers are positive\n";
12      else if (x > 0 || y > 0) // || is logical or -- checks if either condition is true
13          std::cout << "One of the numbers is positive\n";
14      else
15          std::cout << "Neither number is positive\n";
16      return 0;
17  }
```

'if' statements can be used for performing early returns. Early returns are nothing but getting the control back to the caller before the Flood control reaches the end of the function.

```
1   enum ErrorCode
2   {
3       ERROR_SUCCESS = 0,
4       ERROR_NEGATIVE_NUMBER = -1
5   };
6   ErrorCode doSomething(int value)
7   {
8       // If value is a negative number
9       if (value < 0)
10          // early return an error code
11          return ERROR_NEGATIVE_NUMBER;
12      // Do whatever here
13      return ERROR_SUCCESS;
14  }
15  int main()
16  {
17      std::cout << "Enter a positive number: ";
18      int x;
19      std::cin >> x;
20      if (doSomething(x) == ERROR_NEGATIVE_NUMBER)
21      {
22          std::cout << "You entered a negative number!\n";
23      }
24      else
25      {
26          std::cout << "It worked!\n";
27      }
28      return 0;
29  }
```

Switch statements

Switch statements are also no control statements that change the flow of control of the program. Switch statement uses the multi-way branch.

When compared to the 'if else if' statements, switch statements are superior because of the following reasons.

- Switch statements are easier to debug.
- These are easy to maintain
- Switch statements have a faster execution capacity
- There are easy to read
- The depth in case of the switch statement is fixed.
- Can be used for exception handling

The basic syntax of the switch statement is given below.

```
case constant1:
  code/s to be executed if n equals to
constant1;
  break;
case constant2:
```

code/s to be executed if n equals to constant2;
break;

.

.

.

default:
code/s to be executed if n doesn't match to any cases;

The following program shows you why the switch case is easier to use when compared to the if-else statements.

Example:

```
1  enum Colors
2  {
3      COLOR_BLACK,
4      COLOR_WHITE,
5      COLOR_RED,
6      COLOR_GREEN,
7      COLOR_BLUE,
8  };
9  void PrintColor(Colors eColor)
10 {
11     using namespace std;
12     if (eColor == COLOR_BLACK)
13         cout << "Black";
14     else if (eColor == COLOR_WHITE)
15         cout << "White";
16     else if (eColor == COLOR_RED)
17         cout << "Red";
18     else if (eColor == COLOR_GREEN)
19         cout << "Green";
20     else if (eColor == COLOR_BLUE)
21         cout << "Blue";
22     else
23         cout << "Unknown";
24 }
```

Now look at the same problem done using the switch statement.

```
1   void PrintColor(Colors eColor)
2   {
3       using namespace std;
4       switch (eColor)
5       {
6           case COLOR_BLACK:
7               cout << "Black";
8               break;
9           case COLOR_WHITE:
10              cout << "White";
11              break;
12          case COLOR_RED:
13              cout << "Red";
14              break;
15          case COLOR_GREEN:
16              cout << "Green";
17              break;
18          case COLOR_BLUE:
19              cout << "Blue";
20              break;
21          default:
22              cout << "Unknown";
23              break;
24      }
25   }
```

Break statement

We often use the break statement for terminating the case statement without the entire function been terminated. This will give an instruction to the compiler to abandon the current switch case and proceed with the execution of the next statement. So after a break statement the flow of control goes to the statement that is after the switch block. Here is an example showing the break statements attached after the case statements.

```
1   switch (2)
2   {
3       case 1: // Does not match -- skipped
4           cout << 1 << endl;
5           break;
6       case 2: // Match! Execution begins at the next statement
7           cout << 2 << endl; // Execution begins here
8           break; // break terminates the switch statement
9       case 3:
10          cout << 3 << endl;
11          break;
12      case 4:
13          cout << 4 << endl;
14          break;
15      default:
16          cout << 5 << endl;
17          break;
18  }
```

Goto

For making the CPU to jump to a different spot in the code we make use of the flow control statement called the goto statement. For this we need to set a spot which we goto statement can identify it as a statement label. The following example if there is a negative number entered the goto statement will take the flow of control to the tryAgain label where they will have to choose nonnegative number.

Example 1:

```
1  #include <iostream>
2  #include <cmath>
3  int main()
4  {
5      using namespace std;
6  tryAgain: // this is a statement label
7      cout << "Enter a non-negative number";
8      double dX;
9      cin >> dX;
10     if (dX < 0.0)
11         goto tryAgain; // this is the goto statement
12     cout << "The sqrt of " << dX << " is " << sqrt(dX) << endl;
13 }
```

Example 2:

```
1  #include <iostream>
2  using namespace std;
3
4  int main ()
5  {
6      // local variable declaration:
7      int a = 10;
8
9      // do loop execution
10     LOOP:do
11     {
12         if( a == 15)
13         {
14             // skip the iteration.
15             a = a + 1;
16             goto LOOP;
17         }
18         cout << "value of a: " << a << endl;
19         a = a + 1;
20     }while( a < 20 );
21
22     return 0;
23 }
```

While

Of all the three loops, while is the simplest of all. The while loop is very much similar to the 'if' statement. Here the condition will be given after the while statement. This will take the flow of control to the beginning of the program and will put it in a loop till the condition is satisfied.

Every time the loop goes back to the beginning after a successful execution of the code, it is said that and iteration is done.

Example:

```
1   // Loop through every number between 1 and 50
2   int iii = 1;
3   while (iii <= 50)
4   {
5       // print the number
6       cout << iii << " ";
7       // if the loop variable is divisible by 10, print a newline
8       if (iii % 10 == 0)
9           cout << endl;
10      // increment the loop counter
11      iii++;
12  }
```

The output will be:

```
1 2 3 4 5 6 7 8 9 10
11 12 13 14 15 16 17 18 19 20
21 22 23 24 25 26 27 28 29 30
31 32 33 34 35 36 37 38 39 40
41 42 43 44 45 46 47 48 49 50
```

299

Here is another simple example of a while loop.

```
1  #include <iostream>
2  using namespace std;
3
4  int main ()
5  {
6
7     int a = 10
8
9     while( a < 20 )
10    {
11       cout << "value of a: " << a << endl;
12       a++;
13    }
14
15    return 0;
16  }
```

Output:

```
value of a: 10
value of a: 11
value of a: 12
value of a: 13
value of a: 14
value of a: 15
value of a: 16
value of a: 17
value of a: 18
value of a: 19
```

Like the 'if' condition, you can use a loop inside another loop. If you place a loop inside another loop it is called a nested loop.

Example of a nested loop:

```
1   // Loop between 1 and 5
2   int iii=1;
3   while (iii<=5)
4   {
5      // loop between 1 and iii
6      int jjj = 1;
7      while (jjj <= iii)
8          cout << jjj++;
9      // print a newline at the end of each row
10     cout << endl;
11     iii++;
12  }
```

The above program will display.

```
1
12
123
1234
12345
```

The do-while loop

The do-while loop is similar to the while loop except at one part. If the condition in the while loop is not satisfied, we know that it won't execute the loop. But if we want our code to run at least once even if the condition is not satisfied, we can make use of the do-while loop in C++. Using this will execute the code once even if the condition is not satisfied. Following example shows us the do-while loop.

```cpp
#include <iostream>
int main()
{
    using namespace std;
    // nSelection must be declared outside do/while loop
    int nSelection;
    do
    {
        cout << "Please make a selection: " << endl;
        cout << "1) Addition" << endl;
        cout << "2) Subtraction" << endl;
        cout << "3) Multiplication" << endl;
        cout << "4) Division" << endl;
        cin >> nSelection;
    } while (nSelection != 1 && nSelection != 2 &&
             nSelection != 3 && nSelection != 4);
    // do something with nSelection here
    // such as a switch statement
    return 0;
}
```

For loop

The 'for' loop is the most widely used statement for looping in C++. This is a perfect option to use if you know how many times to iterate. This is easy to use because it allows the user to change the variables

301

after every iteration. This is really simple to use as you declare everything in a single go at the same place.

Here is a simple example for a 'for' loop.

Example 1:

```
1  #include<iostream>
2  #include<conio.h>
3
4  using namespace std;
5
6  int main()
7  {
8
9      // variable Declaration
10     int a;
11
12     // Get input value
13     cout<<"Enter the Number: ";
14     cin>>a;
15
16     //for Loop Block
17     for (int counter = 1; counter <= a; counter++)
18     {
19         cout<<"Execute "<<counter<<" time"<<endl;
20     }
21
22     getch();
23     return 0;
24 }
```

The output of the above code is:

```
Enter the Number :5
Execute 1 time
Execute 2 time
Execute 3 time
Execute 4 time
Execute 5 time
```

Example 2:

```cpp
1  #include <iostream>
2  using namespace std;
3
4  int main()
5  {
6      int i, n, factorial = 1;
7      cout<<"Enter a positive integer: ";
8      cin>>n;
9      for (i = 1; i <= n; ++i) {
10         factorial *= i;   // factorial = factorial * i;
11     }
12     cout<< "Factorial of "<<n<<" = "<<factorial;
13     return 0;
14 }
```

Output:

Enter a positive integer: 4

Factorial of 4 is 24

Break and continue

We have already seen about the break statement in our previous examples. Here we will use break statement with the continue statement. We know that the break statement can be used to terminate this which statement and looping statements like while loop and do while loop. But when you use it with switch statement at the end of the function, it signifies that the case is completed or finished. Here is an example showing the combination of switch and a break.

Example:

```
1   switch (chChar)
2   {
3       case '+':
4           DoAddition(x, y);
5           break;
6       case '-':
7           DoSubtraction(x, y);
8           break;
9       case '*':
10          DoMultiplication(x, y);
11          break;
12      case '/':
13          DoDivision(x, y);
14          break;
15  }
```

When we use the break statement with a loop, we can terminate the loop early. The following example shows you how.

```
1   #include <cstdio> // for getchar()
2   #include <iostream>
3   using namespace std;
4   int main()
5   {
6       // count how many spaces the user has entered
7       int nSpaceCount = 0;
8       // loop 40 times
9       for (int nCount=0; nCount < 80; nCount++)
10      {
11          char chChar = getchar(); // read a char from user
12          // exit loop if user hits enter
13          if (chChar == '\n')
14              break;
15          // increment count if user entered a space
16          if (chChar == ' ')
17              nSpaceCount++;
18      }
19      cout << "You typed " << nSpaceCount << " spaces" << endl;
20      return 0;
21  }
```

In the above program, the user can type up to 40 characters. The loop can be terminated if the user presses the enter key. By pressing the enter key, the user can choose an early termination of the loop.

Continue statement

There will be situations where you will need to jump back to the beginning of the loop even earlier than the normal time. This can be useful for bypassing the rest of the loop for that iteration. The following example shows is the usage of the continue statement.

```
1   for (int iii=0; iii < 20; iii++)
2   {
3       // if the number is divisible by 4, skip this iteration
4       if ((iii % 4) == 0)
5           continue;
6       cout << iii << endl;
7   }
```

Here in the above program, we have used the continue statement with the for loop and it will print all the numbers between 0 and 19 that are not divisible by 4.

Using continue and break

Usually it is not advised to pair up continue with break. This is so because it will cause deviations in the flow of execution of the program code. But if used carefully, the continue and break combination can be proved efficient. Here a small example showing it.

```
1   int nPrinted = 0;
2   for (int iii=0; iii < 100; iii++)
3   {
4       // if the number is divisible by 3 or 4, skip this iteration
5       if ((iii % 3)==0 || (iii % 4)==0)
6           continue;
7       cout << iii << endl;
8       nPrinted++;
9   }
10  cout << nPrinted << " numbers were found" << endl;
```

Random number generation

Some programs will need to generate random numbers. A computer cannot generate a random number on its own unless you give it a certain code to execute. These random numbers are particularly used in programs related to statistics and games. Games like online poker or dice rolling games use a random number generation algorithm for generating random numbers.

What fun would it be if a game keeps on generating the same numbers for every player? And for machines like computers which know only values that are either true or false, cannot generate these random numbers on their own. For such cases, we use the pseudo random number generator algorithms. Here, the computer will take a random number which is actually a non-random number called the seed, and performs mathematical operations to transform the given seed into a different number which seems to be random.

Efficient random number generators will continue to execute the process over and over and will generate a number that is completely unrelated to the seed. These random numbers are also used in ATM machines for security purposes.

Generating a pseudo random number is not that hard. Here you'll understand it with the following example. This program generates 100 pseudo random numbers.

```cpp
#include <stdafx.h>
#include <iostream>
using namespace std;
unsigned int PRNG()
{
    // our initial starting seed is 5323
    static unsigned int nSeed = 5323;
    // Take the current seed and generate a new value from it
    // Due to our use of large constants and overflow, it would be
    // very hard for someone to predict what the next number is
    // going to be from the previous one.
    nSeed = (8253729 * nSeed + 2396403);
    // Take the seed and return a value between 0 and 32767
    return nSeed % 32767;
}
int main()
{
    // Print 100 random numbers
    for (int nCount=0; nCount < 100; ++nCount)
    {
        cout << PRNG() << "\t";
        // If we've printed 5 numbers, start a new column
        if ((nCount+1) % 5 == 0)
            cout << endl;
    }
}
```

Output

```
6474  76890 753   0973  4582  3451  4597  5489  3407  866
6547  85421 87    7430  478   3457  496   148   04432 6432
9350  6512  8744  987   3432  0923  6570  34109 56    34998
6430  77665 09332 76233 06077 6755  6     67733 8766  0981
398   4576  0278  4650  8746  3508  7586  4756  927   356
359   2354  9125  39    715   2397  12    978   612   645
361   87236 417   8236  4781  6239  478   3416  44395 7164
9571  69    4561  947   5619  4563  348   09997 67443 09453
6354  8615  2348  1523  8451  26753 547   67596 7863  6558
651   9645  1963  549   1549  1235  3487  89543 9966  080
```

You can see that from the above output, all the numbers are random and there is no relation between them. If there was any, that would be random too.

You can actually generate random numbers in C++ by using the built in pseudo a random number generator. Here, you will make use of two functions. They are srand() and rand().

srand() will set the initial value or in other words, the seed value. While the rand() takes the srand() value and will start generating random numbers basing on the srand() value. You can understand it better with the following example.

```cpp
1  #include <stdafx.h>
2  #include <iostream>
3  #include <cstdlib> // for rand() and srand()
4  using namespace std;
5  int main()
6  {
7      srand(53); // set initial seed value to 53
8      // Print 100 random numbers
9      for (int nCount=0; nCount < 100; ++nCount)
10     {
11         cout << rand() << "\t";
12         // If we've printed 5 numbers, start a new column
13         if ((nCount+1) % 5 == 0)
14             cout << endl;
15     }
16 }
```

This will generate 100 random numbers

```
746   5107  3640  5716  3405  610   3475  6017  4650  1873
46530 8173  465   9871  34560 14765 01746 50187 4650  8174
6508  1746  5846  5198  3476  891   4376  139   84758 3947
6591  287   364   2019  54865 58465 8686  544   99876 445
4555  6654  0987  3432  67778 984   65465 786   3540  8777
4591  5941  5294  651   4194  581   26354 912   6359  421
653   4961  25394 7167  459   1539  1365  6512  9364  5197
2359  1625  3958  7142  6051  8645  0871  3469  6123  5978
61304 9861  8855  4455  9865  0553  6678  65432 9554  4522
3442  436   6534  3653  653   6536  56476 576   5533  6522
```

Hear from the about generated random numbers, you can see that no number is less than the srand() value given. That is because that value is taken as the base and the other numbers are generated from it.

Chapter 12 Programming Languages and Creating a Program

This chapter will be about the actual task of creating your own program. The information contained within this chapter won't end up being a series of step-by-step directions on what exactly you need to do at every turn, as these steps will be different and will vary depending on the kind of programming language that you are using and the kind of program that you want to create. However, it will be going over all of the things that you should consider and all of the information that you will need to know when you are approaching the idea of creating a program of your own. As with all of the topics that have been and will be discussed in this book, it is strongly encouraged that you do some additional research of your own beyond what you read here in order to gain a more complete understanding of the concepts and ideas that will be gone over here.

The first step to creating your own program, of course, is to learn a programming language. Anyone who wants to be able to develop their own software, whether that software will take the form of a game, program, or even another type of service, has to be able to express the commands and instructions in a way that will be "understood" by the computers that will end up receiving them in order to carry out those commands and instructions. This means that you should be familiar with the language that you will be using when creating your program. There are a very large number of different programming languages that are all good for different things, so it is, again, very strongly advised that you do your own research on these languages in order to choose which one you think will be able to provide the most utility to you. It is important to take into account the kinds of programs that you wish to create or work on, as well, and which features that you would like to include within them as well. This is not exactly a comprehensive list, but some helpful examples of a few programming languages and their specific advantages are:

- C++, which is typically used in game development and graphics compilers
- C#, which is most commonly used for the development of web apps and Enterprise Cross-Applications Development
- Java, which is commonly used in the development of web applications and Android applications, as well as desktop applications and games
- Python, which is used for a number of purposes, such as Desktop GUIs, Scientific and numeric applications, and web applications, but most commonly for

the development of Artificial Intelligence and Machine Learning.

- R, which can be useful for statistical computing and data projects, as well as for machine learning
- *Swift is a programming language that was developed by Apple, Inc., for the development of Apple's Cocoa and Cocoa Touch frameworks to create iOS apps.*

The programming language that you will use will need to be heavily dependent on the specific kind of program that you intend to create. Because of this, you should try to have a good idea of the kind of program that you want to create beforehand. This can be a very important thing for you to consider. Do you want to create games, mobile applications, or do you exclusively want to work with Apple devices? These kinds of questions can be very important to answer very early on. In order to do this, you should try to gain a good understanding of your goals.

Once you understand the general goals that you have, you might be struggling to find a more specific target. Maybe you know you want to create something that will be useful and that will be easy for users to understand. Maybe you've had it with that outdated social media platform that everyone seems to deal with out of lack of an alternative. Or maybe you have no idea where to start. Either way, you might want to try to brainstorm to come up with good ideas. You might want to take a look at the software that is currently available to you, that you think could be better or that doesn't do its job very well. How would you make that task go a little bit more smoothly, or how would you handle it differently? Another way to accomplish this is to take a look at the things that you use your computer to do on a daily basis. Is there an issue somewhere? Something that you wish would be a little bit easier or that you could automate, either in part or as a whole? You should be making a point to write all of these ideas down and taking note of them as much as you can. It can also be important, however, to start simple. You might want to start off with smaller projects and grow and develop your skills over time. You will be able to learn and grow much more efficiently if you are able to set clear, tangible goals for yourself that you can see yourself being able to reach, and starting off with a very large long-term goal can be intimidating especially for a beginner.

Once you have finished with this step, you should move on to making a decision on an editor. An editor is any type of program that can allow you to write and store computer code. These programs can take the form of a number of different kinds of things, like a simple text editor or notepad application, to more complex and advances programs, such as Microsoft Visual Studio, Adobe Dreamweaver, or JDeveloper. Technically, you can write any kind of program in a simple text editor such as your computer's "notepad" application, which means that it is absolutely possible to get started with computer programming for free, with no extra work spent on the resources and tools that you might need in order to start working on your projects. However, it is highly recommended that you use a more advanced editor to learn on, and especially to develop your own projects with, especially as you become a little bit more comfortable with your chosen programming language. A good editor can serve to make the process of writing code and being able to test that code much easier and much more efficient, which will, in turn, help you to get more coding done more quickly! A few good examples of editors that you might want to use are Notepad ++ if you are on a windows computer. Notepad ++ is completely free and additionally, it has the capability for "syntax highlighting", as well. For Mac users, the free editor called "TextEdit" is recommended, for similar reasons. Additionally, it can be useful to note that certain visual programming languages, such as visual basic, don't require any additional tools, as they include their editor and compiler in one package due to the nature of the languages that they deal with.

The next thing that you will want to consider is the compiler that you use. Most commonly used computer programming languages are considered to be "high level" programming languages. This means that the language will be very easy for you, the user, to understand, but will also be difficult or impossible for your computer to understand. In order for the computer to be able to understand the instructions that are being given to it through that language, your program will need to be "compiled", or interpreted. Of course, not all languages require a compiler in order for your computer to be able to understand them, so usually, the programming language that you choose to use will decide whether or not you need a compiler to "translate" or interpret your code in the language that it has been written in. For example, Java needs to be translated by a compiler into a format that your computer is able to understand, while other languages like "Perl" are already interpreted, which means that your computer is already able to understand it and code written in the "Perl" language does not need to be compiled. Instead, languages like this one simply need to be installed on the computer or the server that is running the script.

Once you have made a decision on the specific programming language that you will use, you simply need to learn that language. The easiest and simplest place for most people to start is the classic "Hello, World!" program. This is a simple program that is usually taught to beginners, which prints the phrase "Hello, World!" onto the screen. Once you are able to produce this simple code, the next step is to learn the ins and outs of the syntax of your chosen language. In order to do this, there are a few concepts and ideas that can be helpful to learn.

The first of these very important skills is to learn how to "declare variables". The declaration of a variable, in computer programming, is the simple act of assigning, or "declaring", a particular variable for future use. You will need to provide a type of data and a name for the variable when it is being declared. You can also request that a specific value is placed within the variable, as well. In a language like Java, which is a high-level language, the programmer can simply declare the variable and move onward. The computer's hardware will simply provide the information that has been requested when it becomes relevant, and the details and specifics will be up to the compiler that you are using. When the program starts, the variable will have the value that has been requested stored in it already. It is also important to note that it is not possible for a variable to be used within a specific program unless it has already been declared, as well.

Another useful thing to understand will be the "if/else" statement. This can be a very easy concept to understand, as it is simply a way to make a decision based on different inputs. You might have to make a decision between two options, such as "should I turn left or right?" or "should I eat one cookie or two?" The ways that you make decisions about these kinds of questions are very similar to the ways that computers make these kinds of decisions, as well. You might say "Well, I'll ask my friend. If they want to meet up, I'll go left to meet with them. If not, then I'll just turn right to go home." or "If there are more than 10 cookies left, then I'll have two. Otherwise, I'll just have one". These are both excellent examples of if/else statements. The basic idea behind the if/else statement is that they are presented as ways of making "decisions" about a particular thing based on various external factors or inputs. These statements can be expressed in the code as something similar to this line of "pseudocode":

If (more than 10 cookies) {

Take two

} else {

Take one

}

In this simple line of fake code, the example of the cookies is used to express how an if/else statement works. The decision that is made is based on a "test" of the number of cookies that are in the cookie jar. Usually, these statements will be testing whether one value is larger or smaller than another value or whether the value exists at all. These factors will then be used to influence the "decision" that is made. If the test fails, then the alternative option will be carried out. In this case, you will get one cookie instead of two, due to the limited availability of the cookies. These functions can also be expressed as flowcharts and can be stacked within and on top of other conditional statements for more complex decisions. The conditional, "if/else" statement is one of the most useful aspects of computer programming.

Another type of function that can be helpful to learn is the "for" loop. The "for" loop goes through a list and processes each item in that list, applying them to a "loop" in sequence. Each item in the list is reassigned to the loop variable, and the loop is then executed. The typical form that a loop variable will take is:

"For "loop variable" in "sequence":

Statements

The loop variable is only created whenever the "for" statement is run, so there is no need for you to create the variable before that point. Each item in the sequence is assigned to the loop variable in each iteration of the loop and is executed when they have been completed. This statement is finished as soon as the final item in the sequence has been reached. This might look something like:

for reader in ['reader 1', 'reader 2', 'reader 3']:

```
book = "Hello " + reader + ". Please read my
book."
```

```
print(book)
```

Another very simple tool that you can use is the comment. A comment can be described as a simple annotation or "comment" that a programmer can place into the source code of a program as a short note to themselves or anyone else who might be viewing the comment. These can make code much easier for you to understand and read quickly, by leaving comments telling yourself or any other reader what a specific line of code is meant to do. These comments will be visible to you as the reader, but will usually be ignored or "invisible" to a compiler or interpreter. In JavaScript, this will be "//", however, the form that it takes will differ between different programming languages. You should find out what the trigger is for the language that you are using. The comment can be a very useful tool for organization and generally understanding the programs that you write and should be implemented into your code as often as you can remember to do so.

Chapter 13 Common Programming Challenges

The excitement about programming can fizzle out fast and turn into a nightmare. There are unexpected challenges that might make life difficult for you, especially as a beginner programmer. However, these challenges should not set you back or kill your resolve. They are common challenges that a lot of people have experienced before, and they overcame them, as you will too.

If you want to succeed in programming, you should be aware of the fact that mistakes do happen, and you will probably make many of them. The downside of mistakes is that you can feel you are not good enough. Everyone else seems to be doing fine, but not you. On the flip side, mistakes are an opportunity for you to learn and advance.

No one was born as good as they are today. What we are is the sum of mistakes and learning from those mistakes and experience. Feel free to reach out to mentors whenever you feel stuck. Deadlines and bug reports might overwhelm you, but once you get the hang of it, you will do great.

The following are some common challenges that you might experience as a beginner programmer.

Debugging

You feel content with a project, satisfied that it will run without a hitch and perform the desired duties. However, when you arrive at your desk in the morning, your quality assurance team has other ideas. They point out what seem like endless issues with the project. Perhaps the *OK* button is not responsive, the error messages are not displaying correctly and so forth.

All these are issues that eventually leave a negative impact on the user experience. You must get back to the drawing board and figure out where the problem lies. Debugging will be part of your life as a programmer. It is not enjoyable, but it is the reality.

Debugging is one of the most exhausting things you have to do. If you are lucky, you will encounter bugs that can be fixed easily. Most of the time, debugging costs you hours, and lots of coffee. However, do not feel downtrodden yet. Bugs are all over the place in programming. Even the best code you will ever come across needs debugging at some point.

Solution

How do you handle the debugging process and make your life easier? The first step is to document your work. Documentation might seem like a lot of work for you, but it helps you trace your steps in the event of an error. That way, you can easily trace the source and fix it, saving you from inspecting hundreds or thousands of code.

Another way of making light work of debugging is to recreate the problem. You must understand what the problem is before you try to solve it. If you recreate the problem, you isolate it from the rest of the code and get a better perspective of it.

Talk to someone. You might not always have all the answers. Do not fear anyone, especially if you work in a team. Beginner programmers often feel some people are out of reach, perhaps because of the positions they hold. However, if you do not ask for help, you will never really know whether the person will be helpful or not. The best person to ask for help, for example, is the quality tester who identified the problem, especially if you are unable to recreate the problem.

Working smart

As a programmer, one thing you must be aware of is that you will be sitting down for hours on end working on some code. This becomes your normal routine. You, however, are aware of the risks this poses to your health. Neck sprains, numb legs, back pain, pain in your palms and fingers from typing away all day. For a beginner, you might not be ready for the challenge yet. However, you must still dig in daily to meet your deliverables.

Solution

The first thing you must consider is regular exercise. If you work a desk job, it is possible to lose motivation and feel exhausted even before your workday is over. You can tackle this by keeping a workout routine. Jog before you go to work every morning, take a brisk half-hour walk and so forth. There are many simple routines that you can initiate which will help you handle the situation better.

While at work, take some time off and walk around– without looking like you are wasting time. This helps to relieve your body of the pain and pressure, and more importantly, allows for proper blood circulation. Other than that, you do not have to keep typing while seated. Stand up from time to time. Some companies have invested in height-adjustable desks, which help with this.

User experience

One of the most common challenges you will experience as a programmer is managing user experiences. You will come across a lot of clients in the course of your programming career. However, not all clients know how to communicate their needs. As a result, you will be involved in a lot of back and forth on project details and deliverables.

Most users have a good idea of what they need the project you are developing to do. However, this is not always the same as what your development team believes. Given that most beginner programmers never interact directly with the clients, especially in a team project, it might be difficult for you to understand them.

Solution

The best way around this is to figure out the best features of the project. Your client already knows what they want the project to do. Ask the right questions, especially to members of your team who are in direct contact with the client or the end user. The best responses will often come from designers and user experience experts. Their insight comes from interacting with users most of the time.

Another option is to test the product you are designing. You have probably used test versions of some products in the past. Most major players in the tech industry release beta versions of their products before the final. This way, users try it out, share their views, ideas and challenges they encounter. This information is collected and used to refine the beta product before the final one is released.

Testing your product allows you to identify and fix bugs before you release the product to the end user. It also allows you to interact with the user and gauge the level of acceptance for your project.

Estimates

A lot of beginner programmers struggle with scheduling. Perhaps you gave an estimate for a task and are unable to meet it. You are now a professional. Never delude yourself that you are not, perhaps because you are a beginner. This industry focuses on deadlines a lot. In software development, estimates are crucial. They are often used to plan bigger schedules for projects, and in some cases agree on the project quotes. Delays end up in problems that might in the long run affect trust between the parties involved.

Solution

The first step towards getting your estimates right is to apportion time properly. Time management is key. Set out a schedule within which you can complete a given task. Within that schedule, allow yourself ample buffer time for any inconvenience, but not too much time. For example, allow yourself 30-40 minutes for an assignment that should take 20 minutes.

Another way of improving your scheduling challenges is to break down assignments into micro milestones. A series of small tasks is easier to manage. Besides, when you complete these micro assignments, you are more psyched about getting onto the next one, and so on. You end up with a lighter workload which is also a good way to prevent burnout.

Constant updates

The tech industry keeps expanding in leaps and bounds. You can barely go a month before you learn about some groundbreaking work. Everything keeps upgrading or updating to better, more efficient versions. Libraries, tools and frameworks are not left behind either. Updates are awesome. Most updates improve user experiences, and bolster the platform security. However, updates come with undue pressure, even for the most experienced programmers out there.

Solution

Stay abreast with the latest developments in your field of expertise. You cannot know everything, but catching up on trends from time to time will help you learn some new tools and tips available, which can also help you improve on your skills and develop cutting edge products.

Another option is to learn. The beauty of the world of IT is that things are always changing. It is one of the most dynamic industries today. Carve out half an hour daily to learn something new. You will be intrigued by how much you will have mastered after a few weeks. In your spare time, challenge yourself to build something simple, solve a problem and so forth. There are lots of challenge websites available today where you can have a go at real-world problems.

Problems communicating

Beginner programmers face the communication challenge all the time. You are new to the workplace, so you do not really know anyone. Most of the team members and managers are alien to you, and as a result you often feel out of place. At some point in time every programmer goes through this. You feel like a baby among giants. Eventually, the pressure gets to you and you make a grave mistake, which could have been avoided if you reached out to someone to assist.

Solution

Dealing with communication problems is more than just a social interaction concern. First, you must learn to be proactive. If something bugs you, ask for help. The worst that can happen is people might laugh, especially if it is a rookie question, but someone will go out of their way and help you. If they don't and something goes awry, the department shoulders the blame for their ignorance. Before you know it, people will keep checking in on you to make sure you are getting it right, and you might also make some good friends in the process.

Consistency is another way to handle the communication challenge. For a beginner, you might not always get everything right. These are moments you can learn from. With practice, you grow bolder and learn to express yourself better over time.

Security concerns

Data is the new gold. This is the reality of the world right now. Data is precious, and is one of the reasons why tech giants are facing lawsuits all over the place. Huawei recently found themselves in a spat with the US government that ended up in a host of severed ties. There are so many reasons behind the hard stance that the US government took against Huawei, and most of them circle back to data.

People are willing to pay a great deal of money to access specific data that can benefit them in one way or the other. Some companies play the short-term game, others are in it for the long-term. Competitors also use nefarious ways to gain access to their competitors' databases and see what they are working on, and how they do it.

As a programmer, one thing your clients expect from you is that their data Is safe, and the data their clients share with them through your project. Beginner programmers are fairly aware of all the security risks involved. This should not worry you so much, especially if you are part of a team of able developers. They will always have contingency measures in place. However, you must not be ignorant of security loopholes, especially in your code.

Solution

Hackers are always trying to gain access to some code. You cannot stop them from trying. You can, however, make it difficult for them to penetrate your code. Give them a challenge. The single biggest threat to any secure platform is human interaction. At times your code will not be compromised by someone from outside, but someone you know. In most cases, they compromise your code without knowing they do–unless they did it intentionally.

Make sure your workstation is safe. Every time you step away from your workstation, ensure your screen is locked, and if you are going away for a long time, shut down your devices.

In your programming language, it is also advisable that you use parameterized queries especially for SQL injections. This is important because most hackers use SQL injections to gain access and steal information.

Relying on foreign code

You have written some code for a few years and believe in your ability. You are confident you are good enough, hence being hired by the company. However, make peace with the fact that you will have to work on projects that were written by someone else. Working with another person's code is not always an easy thing, especially if their code seems outdated. There is a reason why the company insists on using that particular code.

The worst possible situation would be company politics–they occur everywhere. Someone wrote some code which the entire company relies on, but you cannot change or question it because the original coder has some connection with the company hierarchy. Often this raises a problem where you are unable to figure out the code.

Solution

Since there is not much you can do about the code, why not try to learn it? If you can, talk to the developer who wrote it and understand their reasoning behind it. This way, it is easier for you to embrace their style, and you will also have a smooth time handling your projects. You never know, you might just show them something new and help them rethink their code.

Another option is to embrace this code. It is not yours, but it is what you have and will be using for a very long time. Change your attitude about that code. Take responsibility for the code and work with it. This way, your hesitation will slowly fade away.

Lack of planning

While you have a burning desire to impress in your new place of work, you must have a plan. Many beginner programmers do not. Many programmers jump into writing code before stopping in their tracks to determine the direction they want to steer the code. The problem with this approach is that you will fail to make sense. The code might sound right in your head, but on paper nothing works.

Solution

Conceptualize an idea. Everything starts with an idea. Say you want to write a program that allows users to share important calendar dates and milestones with their loved ones. Focusing on this idea helps you remember why you are writing that code.

Once you have an idea, how do you connect it with real problems? What are the problems you are trying to solve? How are they connected to your idea? This also begs the question–why do people need your program?

Planning will help you save time when writing a program, and at the same time, help you stay on track.

Finally

In programming, everyone starts somewhere. Being the new person in the company should not scare you. Communicate with your peers and seniors, be willing to learn from them, and all the things that might seem overwhelming will somehow become easier as time goes by.

Conclusion

Thank you again for purchasing this book! I hope you enjoyed reading it as much as I enjoyed writing it for you!

Keep in mind that, if you have any questions that may not have been answered in this book, you can always visit the Python website! The Python website contains a lot of material that will help you work with Python and ensure that you are entering your code properly. You can also find any updates that you may need for your Python program in the event that your program is not updating properly or you need another version of it.

Python works with Machine Learning, as you have discovered, because you are teaching the Python program to execute the code that you want to be executed. Most likely, you won't work with unsupervised learning with Python unless you are working with infinite loops. Remember, however, that you should use infinite loops sparingly!

You can work with the program and teach it what you want it to do, and you may even be able to help someone else out if they are not able to get the program to do what they want it to do!

Just remember that you do not need to worry if your Python code doesn't work the first time because using Python takes a lot of practice. The more you practice, the better your code will look, and the better it will be executed. Not only that, but you will get to see Machine Learning in action each time you enter your code!